Breakthrough Prayers For Business Professionals

DR. D. K. OLUKOYA

1st Edition, June 1995
2nd Edition - December, 2003AD
3rd Edition - March, 2010

ISBN 978-32828-0-8

© 2003 AD
A publication of
MOUNTAIN OF FIRE AND MIRACLES MINISTRIES
Press House
13, Olasimbo Street, off Olumo Road,
(By UNILAG Second Gate), Onike, Iwaya
P. O. Box 2990, Sabo, Yaba, Lagos, Nigeria.
Website: www.mountain-of-fire.com
e-mail: mfmhqworldwide@mountainoffire.org

All Scripture quotation is from the King James Version

Cover illustration: Sister Shade Olukoya

CONTENTS

DEDICATION

This Book is dedicated to:

(Late) Brother Abayomi Sogbesan (SAN), an illustrious child of God who dedicated his God-given virtues to the promotion of God's work.

His wife, Sister Abiodun Sogbesan, a dedicated, hardworking and loving woman.

Pastor Kanyi Atiogbe, a wonderful brother and a trusted burden-bearer.

PREFACE

Breakthrough Prayers For Business Professionals is targeted at Christian businessmen who would want to establish and operate their business strictly along biblical principles.

In addition to normal business information such as motivation for going into business, the qualities of a good businessman, etc., the author provides the reader with a comprehensive analysis of the powers that contend in the spiritual realm and how you can protect or deliver your company from their disastrous consequences.

Many business dreams have been aborted at the stage of incubation, some died at infancy. Still, many are collapsing by the day. Why? The reason is that the spirit of Herod is at work.

This book exposes the roles of spiritual gifts in your day-today business operations, divine tips for business success and specially focussed prayers for business breakthroughs.

Finally, it is a practical handbook that has taken due consideration of the peculiarities of the spiritual state of our Environment.

HOW TO USE THIS BOOK

It is time for believers to arise and possess their possessions. A popular gospel hymn says, "O, what needless pains we bear. All because we do not carry everything to God in prayers." The Bible says: "With God all things are possible (Matt. 19:26b)."

This book teaches on how to employ the divine weapons of the Christian to enlarge the coast of his/her business to the glory of God. However, it is important that you read through and understand the messages. The avalanche of messages and prayers included are meant to enable you wrestle your business out of the hands of business killers and plant it in the garden of abundance and prosperity.

Select days of fasting and prayer for your business. It is very helpful to do the praying at the business site if such is available. Some business houses may require spiritual cleansing. This is why the closing message is included. Besides, if you are not a faithful tither, ensure that you make restitution before engaging in the prayer programmes.

1

CHRISTIANS IN BUSINESS

You are welcome to this treasure discovering book, in Jesus' name. The starting point is to state clearly that you don't necessarily have to attend a business school - whether renowned or not, before you become successful in business.

The purpose of going into business must be based on God's prompting or leading which could be via dream, vision or audible voice. As a child of God, you must not be driven into business by any of the under listed presumption / experience / situational demand:

-   You were sacked or retrenched in a former place of work.

-   "I must become my own boss."

-   People say there is monetary gain in it.

-   Someone annoyed you in your former place of work.

- You want fame and popularity.

- Your father is in the same business.

- You think it's an avenue to meet and know people.

- Many people are going into business.

- All my friends are businessmen.

- My wife pressurised me.

- A friend pressurised me.

- I feel that I am very smart.

- I studied Business Administration, Economics and Mathematics.

- It is our family business.

Your basis of going into any business should be on God's instruction.

"Where He leads, I go," says a popular song. However, many have changed it to "Where I go, He must follow." You cannot construct your own foundations outside God and then invite Him to complete the building. The truth is that God will not build on a foundation that He didn't begin.

Once you know that God instructed you to start a particular business, then, there is no reason why you should not become prosperous.

You must understand that the business world is a world of

- intricate deception

- cruelty

- sweet talkers

- unrighteous diplomacy

- self-abuse

- compromises

- set-backs

- disappointments

- charms

- frustration

- risks

- demonic manipulations

So, you must be sure that you heard from the Lord before going into it.

THE QUALITIES OF A GOOD CHRISTIAN BUSINESSMAN

The underlisted abilities or qualities are essential tools for any business engagement. Perhaps you are in business and you discover that you lack one or more of these qualities, then, you must pray aggressively.

Power to take initiative

- Do you depend on others to take the initiative or prompt them to do so?

- Do you look for things that need to be done or wait for others to find out?

- Do you do things that need to be done before being asked by others to do so?

- Do you like challenges and new opportunities?

- Do you hate trying new things or only prefer activities you know very well?

If your answers to the above are NO, then you need to pray about the power to take initiative - with the right finesse governed by the Holy Spirit.

A good businessman should be able to take initiative and not be like the doubter in the book of James, chapter 1, verses 5 and 6: If any of you lack wisdom, let him ask of God, that giveth to all men liberally, and upbraideth not; and it shall be given him. But let him ask in faith, nothing wavering. For he that wavereth is like a wave of the sea driven with the wind and tossed.

Ability to persist

Persistence means: Ability to take repeated or different actions to overcome an obstacle. Further more, it is the ability to keep on trying in the face of opposition or early lack of success.

Ask yourself these questions:

- When faced with a difficult problem, do you spend a lot of time trying to find a solution?

- Do you easily give up when things do not work the way you want?

- Do you enjoy finding solution to a problem?

- When faced with major difficulties, do you quickly go on to other things?

Your answers will determine how persistent you are. If you are a quitter, you will never be a good businessman. Suffice it to say that you may not succeed. Remember, quitters don't ever win and winners don't ever quit.

Those who jump from one thing to the other without staying long enough on any particular one are quitters. To be successful, you have to be like the woman in the book of Luke, chapter 18, verses 1 to 5:

> And He spake a parable unto them to this end, that men ought always to pray, and not to faint; Saying, There was in a city a judge, which feared not God, neither regarded man: And there was a widow in that city; and she came unto him, saying, Avenge me of mine adversary. And he would not for a while: but afterward he said within himself, Though I fear not God, nor regard man; Yet because this widow troubleth me, I will avenge her, lest by her continual coming she weary me.

Many successful business people did not succeed the first time, but they persisted until success came.

Power to seek information

This is the ability to go out and seek information on clients, suppliers, available markets and competitors.

- Do you gather a great deal of information before going ahead to start a new task or project?

- Do you seek the advice of people who know a lot about what you are working on?

- Do you take action without taking time to gather information?

- Do you go to several different sources to get information before beginning on a task or project?

- Do you confirm that there is a lucrative market for what you propose to sell?

A man wants to set up a ping-pong centre, he goes to those who have been operating it. Finds out the cost of the table, light, bats and the plastic ball. He does a statistics of the number of interested children in the area. Finds out from the kids their level of interest. Finds out how many of such playing centres are in the neighbourhood. Such is the wise step into success.

If you are not the information-seeking type, then you qualify for the position of the kind of man and the king described by Jesus in the book of Luke, chapter 14, verses 28 to 32:

> *For which of you, intending to build a tower, sitteth not down first, and counteth the cost, whether he have sufficient to finish it? Lest haply, after he hath laid the foundation, and is not able to finish it, all that behold it began to mock him, Saying, This man began to build, and was not able to finish. Or what king, going to make war against another king, sitteth not down first, and consulteth whether he be able with ten thousand to meet him that cometh against him with twenty thousand? Or else, while the other is yet a great way off, he sendeth an ambassage, and desireth conditions of peace.*

Power to excel

This is the ability to do things that meet or exceed existing standards of excellence; to improve on past performances; to strive to do things better; to strive to excel; to strive to do things faster and cheaper.

However,

- Does it bother you when things are not done well or you really don't mind?

- Do you strive to make your work better than those of others?

- Do you seek ways of improving what you are doing to make it outstanding?

A good businessman will pursue and work towards the biblical injunction: Deut. 28:13, Prov. 22:29:

> *And the LORD shall make thee the head, and not the tail; and thou shalt be above only, and thou shalt not be beneath; if that thou hearken unto the commandments of the LORD thy God, which I command thee this day, to observe and to do them.*

> *Seest thou a man diligent in his business? he shall stand before kings; he shall not stand before mean men.*

It is the mark of failure if you no longer seek to improve and beat others at what you are doing.

Power of soundness

The power of soundness is the ability to develop and use logical step by step plans to reach goals. It is also the ability to evaluate alternative ways of doing things.

Consider the following:

- Do you plan a large project by breaking it down into smaller tasks?

- Do you think about the advantages or disadvantages of different ways of accomplishing things?

- Do you try to plan solutions to problems that may arise?

- Do you deal with problems as they arise or spend time trying to anticipate what to do if they arise?

- Do you find it difficult to follow a plan or schedule?

Then, you are running a business on limited oil like the five foolish virgins who did not anticipate that the oil might finish.

Matt. 25:1-10:

> *"Then shall the kingdom of heaven be likened unto ten virgins, which took their lamps, and went forth to meet the bridegroom. And five of them were wise and five were foolish. They that were foolish took their*

lamps, and took no oil with them: But the wise took oil in their vessels with their lamps. While the bridegroom tarried, they all slumbered and slept. And at midnight there was a cry made, Behold, the bridegroom cometh; go ye out to meet him. Then all those virgins arose, and trimmed their lamps. And the foolish said unto the wise, Give us of your oil; for our lamps are gone out. But the wise answered, saying, Not so; lest there be not enough for us and you: but go ye rather to them that sell, and buy for yourselves. And while they went to buy, the bridegroom came; and they that were ready went in with him to the marriage: and the door was shut."

They did not put aside extra oil. It is like driving a vehicle without a spare tyre. Such people do not make good businessmen.

Power of confidence

This is the power to have a strong belief in your God-given ability and to express confidence in your ability to complete a difficult task or meet a challenge.

Ponder on the following:

- Do you always feel confident that you will succeed at whatever you try to do, no matter how difficult?

- Do you easily change your mind on a business venture when others strongly disagree with you?

- Are you always confident that you will perform well?

If this confidence is lacking, or you are always feeling inferior, then, you need to pray.

You need to be able to declare like Isaiah in Isaiah 50:7:

> *For the Lord God will help me; therefore shall I not be confounded: therefore have I set my face like a flint, and I know that I shall not be ashamed.*

The power of violent faith

This is the ability to engage in situations that have a high risk, as opposed to taking a preference for situations involving moderate risk. It is also being bold enough to take some steps into the dark - going the extra mile.

Ruminate on the following:

- Do you prefer situations in which you can control the outcome as much as possible?

- Are you the type who will not try anything new without first making sure it will succeed?

- Do you weigh your chances of succeeding or failing before you decide to do something?

- Do you do things that are risky?

- Do you do things that others consider risky?

- Are you risk averse?

Success sometimes involves taking risks. There is a risk in not taking risks. The Christian life of faith is sometimes a decision to take a step in the dark. Fear looks, faith jumps. Men of faith in the Bible were men who took holy risks.

Until the priests stepped on Jordan river, the waters did not divide.

He that observeth the winds shall not sow; and he that regardeth the clouds shall not reap. Eccl. 11:4.

Power of persuasion

The power of persuasion is the ability to influence and persuade others. In addition, it is the ability to use personal and social contacts to accomplish one's objectives.

Note the points below:

- Do you have ways of getting others to support your recommendations?

- Do you spend much time thinking about how to influence others?

- Do you get important people to help you accomplish your goals.

- Are you able to get people who have strong opinions or ideas to change their minds?

The power of persuasion is an important tool for the businessman.

Nehemiah was able to persuade men to assist in building the broken walls of Jerusalem. Neh. 2:17,18:

> "Then said I unto them, Ye see the distress that we are in, how Jerusalem lieth waste, and the gates thereof are burned with fire: come, and let us build

up the wall of Jerusalem, that we be no more a reproach. Then I told them of the hand of my God which was good upon me; as also the king's words that he had spoken unto me. And they said, Let us rise up and build. So they strengthened their hands for this good work.

Power of commitment

The power of commitment is the ability to be faithful to a cause.

Examine the questions below:

- Do you complete your work on time?

- Do you keep the promises you make?

- Are you happy to do someone else's work to get the job done in time?

- When you are working for someone, do you make special effort to ensure that the person is happy with your work?

Commitment to fulfilling promises is another essential tool. Your Yes, must be Yes and your No, must be No: Your stand point must be clearly defined. Your 'almost finished' must be 90 per cent finished and not 50 per cent.

Listen to the words of the Lord Jesus Christ in Matt. 5:37:

> *"But let your communication be, Yea, yea; Nay, nay: for whatsoever is more than these cometh of evil."*

Power of vision

This is simply setting a standard for yourself. Moreso, it is defining the goals that you would like to attain.

Reflect your mind on these questions:

*   Do you like to think about the future of what you are doing? .

*   Do you have a very clear plan of the goals to attain?

*   Do you set weekly goals and yearly goals or do you just work on without a goal?

In life, setting a goal is necessary. Thus, as Christians, we are not excluded.

When there is a goal before you, then you have a vision of what you want to attain. Phil. 3:10-14 says:

> *That I may know Him, and the power of His resurrection, and the fellowship of His suffering,*

being made conformable unto His death; If by any means I might attain unto the resurrection of the dead. Not as though I had already attained, either were already perfect: but I follow after, if that I may apprehend that for which also I am apprehended of Christ Jesus. Brethren, I count not myself to have apprehended: but this one thing I do, forgetting those things which are behind, and reaching forth unto those things which are before. I press toward the mark for the prize of the high calling of God in Christ Jesus.

Jesus is the way. The way is not the destination. The destination or goal is the Father.

Moreso, is the necessity of **virtue**, which a good business person must possess. It includes qualities such as integrity/honesty, prudence, courage, etcetera. Integrity/honesty creates the foundation of trust while courage is needed to face the vicissitudes of business.

If you lack any of these essential abilities, you would have to pray about it or make corrections.

Having identified these abilities, we now move to a very important area.

SPIRITUAL GIFTS

One neglected area by Christian businessmen is that of the gift of the Spirit. (I Cor. 12:7-11.) Believers should be aware that the Holy Spirit is interested in affecting every part of our lives. God wants to help us with every part of our lives, whether public or private and He wants to bless our lives beyond our wildest imaginations.

The Bible says we should desire spiritual gifts, (I Cor. 14:1).

There are three types of revelational gifts to know a particular thing supernaturally. These are:

Word of Knowledge - Examples: Prophet Elisha used it to locate Gehazi (2Kings 5:20-27). It was used to know the location of the Syrian army whenever they laid ambush for the Israelites (2Kings 6:8-14). Paul knew the future of the troubled ship through it (Acts 27:21-24).

Word of Wisdom - Through this gift, Jesus stupefied the Jews who were about to stone the woman caught in act of adultery (John 8:1-11).

Discerning of spirits - Paul discerned that the girl crying after him and Silas was not of God (Acts 16:16-19). With this gift in operation, people's mind could be read.

If Christian businessmen would get filled with the Holy Ghost and receive any or all of the three gifts above, they would become very prosperous. The Spirit of God could tell you where to buy an item cheaply, when and where to invest your money. The Spirit of God could also tell you when a particular business is genuine and when it is not.

Through the three gifts of revelation, we may know anything that God chooses to reveal by His Spirit. These three gifts enable God to do exploits through His people and win supernatural battles over satan.

Spiritual gifts are not only for pastors, evangelists and other ministers. They are for believers, whether they are drivers, carpenters, farmers, tailors or traders. These gifts are irrespective of believers' profession or vocation.

These gifts would come upon those who present themselves as living sacrifice to God.

The gift of the Word of Knowledge can tell the conditions or whereabouts of a particular thing when it is not possible to learn it in the natural. The gift enables you to know things even when you do not pray about them. Although its purpose is to find lost souls and populate heaven, it has helped to find lost articles and to get useful information.

God can make you know where the right customers are, and the character and nature of a customer. He is concerned with every detail about our lives. He can show you areas of profitable operations in dreams, visions or through an audible voice.

When you have received such supernatural revelations, then you would know better how to pray.

The Word of Wisdom is also a wonderful gift to desire. It is God showing the How, Why, When, Where and What of a matter.

Whatever vocation you are involved in, you need this gift.

It is a gift every businessman should possess. It would enable him/her to solve problems that arise in business. Every businessman needs a Word of Wisdom nearly every day.

Solomon in the Bible faced a dilemma when two women quarrelled about the parenthood of a child (1 Kings 3:16-28). Paul the Apostle was in a tight corner several times. This wonderful gift always helped him out.

Many businesses collapse because of lack of divine wisdom for guidance.

Discerning of spirits is another wonderful gift that is seriously needed. You know immediately which spirit is in operation and then, take action.

With this gift, you can discern who to trust, who to work with. You can choose proper workers and not those who will dupe your company. We need to be able to discern the spirits operating at business meetings.

The gift of Faith and Working of Miracles is also useful for those who are in business.

Releasing yourself completely to the Power of the Holy Ghost and operating Spiritual Gifts will make you a highly successful businessman.

BUSINESS KILLERS

There are some powers that we call "Business Killers."

Below, is a list and analysis of the various, afore-mentioned business killers.

Wrong partnership

We cannot bless whom God has cursed. You cannot expect

God to bless your business when your partner is an enemy of God or is occultic, who when you are praying, he is offering sacrifices. God would just fold His hands. (2 Cor. 6:14-18, 1 Cor. 15:33, James 4:4).

If you cannot get a Christian partner, then go alone in the business. It is better to get a Christian partner, otherwise, go alone into the business.

Anti-prosperity forces

They are:

* Unfaithfulness with tithes and offerings.

* Not sowing seed into God's work.

* Employment of demonised people.

* Sacrificing fellowship time for business.

* Operation of dishonest business.

* Attack by devourers.

* Attack by demonic forces.

* Attack by fire or thieves.

Starting a business on a wrong motive

- Have you obtained a go-ahead from the Lord?

- Or are you in business because you want independence, power or position?

  If your motive is not right, the business will collapse.

Lack of ability

- What skills do you possess?

- What do you know about the business you are running?

- Have you taken time to understand the technicalities of the business or you depend on your employees to tell you what is going on?

- Do you have any managerial experience or talent?

  Lack of ability will kill the business.

Wrong choice of business

- You must pray and receive information from the Lord on the choice of business.

- It is better for you to seek God's face before you start than to start and lament your failure afterwards.

  This is an important stage and it does not matter how long it takes.

Lack of resources

- You must prayerfully seek out the resources. It may be cash, raw materials, machinery, equipment or labour.

  Without the necessary resources the business will collapse.

Owing large debts

You must pray through before you take large loans. It is not God's will for you to borrow bloody money to start your business.

If you must take a loan, be sure that God has told you which, how, when and where.

In fact, the Bible says: "Owe no man anything," Romans 13:8.

Laziness

No progress can be made on any physical and spiritual thing by a lazy person. Laziness is not condoned by God hence He wouldn't have created man to till or work the ground (Gen. 2:5).

TIPS FOR SUCCESS

1. Be sure you are following God's directives.

2. Be filled with the Holy Ghost.

3. Locate your weakness or lack and pray over it.

4. Disengage yourself from unprofitable partners.

5. Pray off anti-prosperity forces.

6. Be generous towards God.

7. Sow heavily into God's vineyard.

8. Be kind to the needy.

9. Learn the principles of staying in divine health.

10. Pray about and practise increasing your power of concentration.

11. Pray about improved memory.

12. Be a good listener and resist talkativeness.

13. Let God be the head of your home.

14. Be humble.

PRESCRIPTIONS FOR SUCCESS

Learn the alphabets of success.

A   ACTION - Even so faith, if it hath not works, is dead, being alone (James 2:17).

B   BELIEF - But without faith it is impossible to please Him: for he that cometh to God must believe that He is, and He is a rewarder of them that diligently seek Him (Heb. 11:6).

C   COMMITMENT - Whatsoever thy hand findeth to do, do it with thy might; for there is no work, nor device, nor knowledge, nor wisdom, in the grave, whither thou goest (Eccl. 9:10).

D   DIRECTION - I therefore so run, not as uncertainly; so fight I, not as one that beateth the air (1 Cor. 9:26).

E ENTHUSIASM - Seest thou a man diligent in his business? He shall stand before kings; he shall not stand before mean men (Prov. 22:29).

F FAITH - But Jesus beheld them, and said unto them, With men this is impossible; but with God all things are possible (Matt. 19:26).

G GOALS - Know ye not that they which run in a race run all, but one receiveth prize? So run, that ye may obtain (1 Cor. 9:24).

H HAPPINESS - Therefore with joy shall ye draw water out of the wells of salvation (Isa. 12:3).

I INSPIRATION - The Spirit of the Lord is upon me, because He hath anointed me . . .(Luke 4:18).

J JUDGEMENT - For God hath not given us the spirit of fear; but of power, and of love, and of a sound mind (2 Tim. 1:7).

K KNOWLEDGE - The fear of the Lord is the beginning of wisdom: and the knowledge of the holy is understanding (Prov. 9:10).

L   **LOVE** - Charity never faileth: but whether there be prophecies, they shall fail; whether there be tongues, they shall cease; whether there be knowledge, it shall vanish away (1 Cor. 13:8).

M   **MOTIVATION** - Who, when he came, and had seen the grace of God, was glad, and exhorted them all, that with purpose of heart they would cleave unto the Lord (Acts 11:23).

N   **NON-CONFORMITY** - Be ye not unequally yoked together with unbelievers: for what fellowship hath righteousness with unrighteousness? and what communion hath light with darkness? (2 Cor. 6:14).

O   **OBEDIENCE** - And Samuel said, Hath the LORD as great delight in burnt offerings and sacrifices, as in obeying the voice of the LORD? Behold, to obey is better than the fat of rams (1 Sam. 15:22).

P   **PERSISTENCE** - For a just man falleth seven times, and riseth up again: . . .(Prov. 24:16).

Q   **QUALITY** - And the Lord shall make thee the head, and not the tail; and thou shalt be above only, and thou shalt not be beneath; . . .(Deut. 28:13)

R   RIGHTEOUSNESS - For I say unto you, That except your righteousness shall exceed the righteousness of the scribes and Pharisees, ye shall in no case enter into the kingdom of heaven (Matt. 5:20).

S   STEADFASTNESS - Therefore, my beloved brethren, be ye steadfast, unmoveable, always abounding in the work of the Lord, forasmuch as ye know that your labour is not in vain in the Lord (1 Cor. 13:58).

T   THANKFULNESS - Giving thanks always for all things unto God and the Father in the name of our Lord Jesus Christ; (Eph. 5:20).

U   UNIQUENESS - But ye are a chosen generation, a royal priesthood, an holy nation, a peculiar people; that ye should shew forth the praises of Him who hath called you out of darkness into His marvellous light: (1 Pet.2:9).

V   VISION - Where there is no vision, the people perish: but he that keepeth the law, happy is he (Prov. 29:18).

W   WISDOM - Buy the truth, and sell it not; also wisdom, and instruction, and understanding (Prov. 23:23).

X **eXCELLENCE** - O LORD Our Lord, how excellent is Thy name in all the earth! who hast set Thy glory above the heavens (Psalm 8:1).

Y **YIELDNESS** - Submit yourselves therefore to God. Resist the devil, and He will flee from you (James 4:7).

Z **ZEAL** - For the zeal of thine house hath eaten me up; and the reproaches of them that reproached thee are fallen upon me (John 2:17).

2

SWALLOWERS OF PROSPERITY

Psalm 1:1-3: Blessed is the man that walketh not in the counsel of the ungodly, nor standeth in the way of sinners, nor sitteth in the seat of the scornful. ²But his delight *is* in the law of the LORD; and in his law doth he meditate day and night. ³And he shall be like a tree planted by the rivers of water, that bringeth forth his fruit in his season; his leaf also shall not wither; and whatsoever he doeth shall prosper.

By now, you would have agreed with me that poverty is devastating. I personally have decided to hate it and be its enemy forever. The person who has never in his life prospered, and the one whose prosperity was swallowed, are the same.

Prosperity - This is the state of being in the centre of God's purpose for your life. Prosperity could be said to mean:

- Blessings from God.

- Ability to meet one's and other people's needs sufficiently.

- Having no difficultly in financial or physical obligations to the society - home, church, company, etc.

BIBLE PROSPERITY

This refers to using our God given ability and knowledge to meet needs - whether physical or spiritual. Jesus did not need to carry money about but He never lacked, and He blessed people everywhere He went.

Bible prosperity also means having adequate provision to meet up with God's plans for one's life (I Tim. 5:8).

Ecclesiastes 5:19: Every man also to whom God hath given riches and wealth, and hath given him power to eat thereof, and to take his portion, and to rejoice in his labour; this *is* the gift of God.

This means that getting riches and wealth as well as the power to eat them and be happy is a gift from God. The Bible says: "Ask and it shall be given unto you, seek and ye shall find . . . (Matt. 7:7)."

Therefore, wretchedness is not from God. Abraham, Joseph, Daniel, etc were not poor and are in heaven. The onus is on the children of God to ask Him for an all round blessing to glorify His name.

A long time ago, a tax assessor went to a pastor to assess his possessions. The pastor had only three old chairs in his sitting room and a centre table. The tax assessor asked him where his property was and he answered that it was in heaven.

He had everlasting life, a mansion in heaven, peace that passes all understanding, joy unspeakable, healthy body, divine love that would never cease and a crown of life awaiting him. The tax collector was dumbfounded and agreed that he was really rich but that his wealth could not be assessed and therefore not taxable.

If you have Christ, you need nothing more. Problems come when people don't possess Christ fully and don't allow Him to possess them. God is the source of prosperity.

The Bible says: "A man can receive nothing, except it be given him from heaven" (John 3:27). A lot of people receive their own prosperity from beneath. God, the author of prosperity, made the earth and planted the gold and all other minerals, crude oil, and everything in its bowels.

Every child of God should pray hard to be prosperous. Unfortunately, poverty is not a passport to heaven. In fact, there are many rich people in hell now, just as there are many poor ones there as well.

There is a demon of poverty which tortures people on earth and such people still end up in hell. Pray like this: *Every stronghold of poverty, I smash you to nothingness, in the name of Jesus.*

There is an anointing of poverty which makes a place that was once prosperous become nothing, as soon as a certain possessor or occupant moves in. Many businesses close up because somebody with the anointing of poverty was employed.

Some time ago, I went to a supermarket and the Lord opened my eyes to see that the girl distributing tickets at the entrance was a mermaid. The whole of her body was fish. I was sorry for the owner of the supermarket because I knew that all the money made there would be taken spiritually into the waters.

I was not surprised when the supermarket closed down after a while. This happened because the legs of poverty walked into it. Whereas, the Bible says: "how beautiful are the feet of them that preach the gospel . . ." (Romans 10:15). If there are beautiful feet, there are ugly ones too.

Pray like this: *Every ugly foot, walk out of my business, in the name of Jesus.*

If after this prayer, any of your employees resigns, allow him or her to go. The Christian is privileged above others.

Pray this prayer: *I will rise above all the unbelievers around me, in the name of Jesus.*

Christians are more entitled to the good things of life than other people, but there is a problem: God finds it difficult to entrust his money into the hands of many Christians. Can He trust you? Will you remain fervent if you become rich? Perhaps, the prayer that most Christians should be praying is that the Lord should break them, rather than asking for money or prosperity.

You must get to the level where prosperity cannot affect the level of your brokenness. Then, God will bless you to a dumbfounding degree.

Kinds of Prosperity

- Material

- Spiritual

- Health

Prosperity without health or spiritual soundness is nothing.

Beloved, I wish above all things that thou mayest prosper and be in health, even as thy soul prospereth (III John 2).

SWALLOWERS OF PROSPERITY

Inordinate love of money

Your attitude to money is very important to God; you must examine yourself. God is a God of wisdom; if you are a person that picks money on the ground, if you tell lies to get money, then you have to change.

Paul said: "The love of money is the root of all evil (I Tim. 6:10)." If a person loves money in a crude way, he/she is ready to do anything to obtain money.

Indications of inordinate love of money are as follows:

* ***Exaggerated importance placed on money and money matters.*** This happens if losing money or lack of it makes a person depressed or develop suicidal tendencies.

- **Thinking that money can do or buy everything**. Note, money can buy a bed but cannot buy sleep or rest. It can buy books but not intelligence.

- **Bowing to unscriptural circumstances and conforming to the image of the world because of money**.

Once you sort these things out, the Lord will bless you. Some people think they can borrow their tithe and even quote scriptures in an attempt to justify their wrong actions. The truth is that when you borrow tithes, you have to pay them back with 15 per cent interest and the initial benefits are suspended.

Pray like this: *Anything in my life, that will make God withhold His prosperity, get out now, in the name of Jesus.*

When I was in the primary school, our teacher told us a story of a man who ran into a village, shouting: "Death, death" and some villagers followed him. When they got to the bush, they saw the corpses of three hunters on the ground and a bag of money in their midst.

What happened? They were going about hunting for animals, when they found a bag of money and decided to share it. They decided to eat some food first. One of them volunteered to go and buy the food. As he went the other two conspired to kill him and have the money for themselves. The one who went to buy the food also decided to poison the food and not eat it, so that the other two would eat and die and he would have the money to himself alone.

At the sight of the one that went to buy food, the other two shot him. Then, they ate the food and as soon as they finished eating they died - that is the irony of life.

Money is capable of appearing as good or as evil. When you notice a spirit within you that wants to get rich at all cost, you have to be careful. You will either rule money or it will rule you.

It does not matter whether you are rich or poor, you could be ruled by money. The love of money makes drivers reckless, as they want to make as many trips as possible. It makes men go into the occult hence, their life span is shortened. It makes people kill one another.

Many Christians abandon God and toil for money, even on Sundays. Many sell their bodies for money. But any money got from affliction and sin leads to more problems - this is the basic truth.

A primary school teacher of mine recounted another story. In a village, a meeting was called and people did not turn up. The chairman of the occasion was Mr. Death. The following day, Mr. Money offered to come along. When people saw that money was involved, they came.

Some kinds of money will remove good things from the life of a person and even destroy his life.

A pastor inherited two houses from his mother and put them out for rent. When he collected the rent and put it into his account, he started having financial problems. He prayed fervently and God revealed to him that he was collecting blood money and was adding it to his own. His mother was demonic, so also was the money from her house.

Pray like this: *Any strange money that has entered into my hands, go away, in the name of Jesus.*

It is because God knows that some people have certain things or money which belong to other people in their possession that the Bible talks about restitution.

Until some people restitute, they may not have their own real prosperity. If you have ever stolen things from your employer, you have to restitute. If the company has folded up, restitute to God. If you stole anything from a country abroad or you bought things with your credit card and ran away, you have to restitute.

Leviticus 6:1-4: And the LORD spake unto Moses, saying, [2]If a soul sin, and commit a trespass against the LORD, and lie unto his neighbour in that which was delivered him to keep, or in fellowship, or in a thing taken away by violence, or hath deceived his neighbour; [3]Or have found that which was lost, and lieth concerning it, and sweareth falsely; in any of all these that a man doeth, sinning therein: [4]Then it shall be, because he hath sinned, and is guilty, that he shall restore that which he took violently away, or the thing which he hath deceitfully gotten, or that which was delivered him to keep, or the lost thing which he found.

You have to take stock of the things that are in your possession and return that which is not yours. If you paid someone for two things and you took three, you have to return one.

Why restitute?

Habakkuk 2:6: Shall not all these take up a parable against him, and a taunting proverb against him, and say, Woe to him that increaseth *that which is* not his! how long? and to him that leadeth himself with thick clay!

This is where prosperity swallowers wait for some people.

A sister came for prayers on marital breakthrough. As we were praying, the Lord opened my eyes and I saw a lot of gifts packed in one place. I opened my eyes and asked if she had ever been engaged to any man.

She said many. I asked if she ever took anything from them and she said yes. She said she locked up all the gifts from the men she jilted in a room in her flat. This is a ground on which the enemy would accuse her. God wants you to sort out things like this before you move ahead.

A brother learnt about restitution and decided to return the two pumping machines he had stolen from his place of work before he became a Christian. He had already fixed one in his house. On his way to the office with the machines, a voice told him to go back and sell the machines and put the money on the director's table so that it would not be known that it was he that stole them earlier on.

But the Spirit of God convinced him to go ahead and give the director those machines, and he went on. The director was impressed and congratulated him on his courage and honesty. That incident earned him promotion instead of being given a sack.

If the brother had not done that and was praying for prosperity, the devil would have continually accused him before God and it would have hindered his blessings.

Pray like this: *O Lord, break me down to the level where you can trust me with your riches, in the name of Jesus.*

Wealth of Sorrow

Proverbs 10:22: The blessing of the LORD, it maketh rich, and he addeth no sorrow with it.

There is a blessing from God and there is also a counterfeit blessing from the devil. If you look through the Bible, you will find that the devil wants to have a duplicate of every good thing. You will find God's doctrines in it and also the doctrines of demons. You will find the table and cup of God, and those of the devil.

There are apostles of Christ, and the devil has his own too. There is fellowship with the Lord and worship with the devil. Whilst the blessings of God make a person rich and happy, the counterfeit blessings of the devil impoverish and bring sorrow.

Wealth of sorrow is anything acquired through unrighteous or dubious means or profit, extortion, bribe, stealing, etc.

In some families, when a man dies, relatives fight over his property, neglecting the widow and the children. Such people never prosper. Some people steal from accident victims who are dead. Some steal properties of fire victims, they cannot prosper with such things.

Anyone who sells fake or expired drugs cannot prosper. Injustice meted out to the innocent brings curse on the judge and lawyer. Killing a person physically or with charms and taking over his position or wealth only brings about curses. False acquisition of property, cheating widows, orphans and children or defrauding ignorant people, is wealth of sorrow.

This is why sometimes, when a person surrenders his life to Christ, He turns him upside down and shakes off the ill-gotten wealth in him, so that he can acquire a new one from God.

The drive for quick wealth and the ability to do anything to acquire wealth, brings sorrow. It cannot be combined with proper wealth from God. If you exploit your employees to get wealth, you are acquiring wealth of sorrow.

Although, this category of people may appear successful or wealthy in the eyes of the world, yet this ill-gotten wealth is a squalid distortion of God's instruction.

Pray like this: *Any power scaring away my prosperity, fall down and die, in the name of Jesus.*

Wicked Stubborn Pursuers

A woman prayed to get married and got a man. But the man came a few days to the wedding and said he was no longer interested because the woman was too short. A second man came and a few days to the wedding died in an accident.

A third one came and on the day of the wedding, as the reverend asked the normal question, if anyone had anything against the marriage, a woman signified and came forward with two children and a marriage certificate which was issued abroad. The man was her husband.

The sister almost died. She was not born again then. Later, she gave her life to Christ and during the deliverance session the secret of her wicked, stubborn pursuers was revealed to her.

If you sleep and wake up without problems, you should thank God, because there are many people who cannot sleep because of the nightmares they always experience.

As a deliverance minister, I have discovered that many people have been suffering in the hands of wicked, stubborn pursuers who would not want to let go their preys. They speak out that they have legal rights over their preys.

One day, as I was praying for a brother, I saw a woman holding his leg in one hand and a coffin in the other. I described the person to him and he said it was a lady he jilted years ago. As I was about to continue to pray for him, the Lord told me not to bother because he was already a dead man. He actually died a week later.

If a person's finances are being pursued, he will find that his business is having problems. He will discover that where people had been helpful before, he is rejected. Such a person struggles and works hard but there is nothing to show for it. Every good thing he does for people is repaid with evil. When he has goods in his shop, they will be there until they go bad or are auctioned.

All these are the threats of wicked, stubborn pursuers. I pray that such enemies in your life will be disgraced today.

If you find yourself seeing dead relatives, bats, serpents, naked people, armed robbers, etc. in the dream, then, you should know that you are being pursued. You may not have known these things before, but this message affords you an opportunity to do so.

Pray like this: *Woe unto every wicked vessel pursuing my prosperity, in the name of Jesus.*

If you know that every area seems to be working except your finances, then you will take the following steps:

- **Prayerfully review your past life.**

    Have you entered into any evil covenants consciously or unconsciously? Have you had sexual relationship with a possessed person? Do you have a history of childhood failures? Have you ever been cursed by your parents or anyone else?

    Have you ever gone to seek help from a charmer, herbalist, white-garment prophet? Have you ever eaten anything sacrificed to idols? Have you ever gone through an abortion or assist anyone in carrying it out? Have you ever been in an occult group?

Was your father occultic? Was he a herbalist or a, polygamist? Are you a polygamist or an adulterer? Were you bed-wetting as a child? Have you ever jilted a fiancé or fiancee?

Are you unfaithful to a loving spouse? Are there any traits of poverty in your family line? Have you ever stolen money or anything? Have you ever used any occultic means to look for money?

If you are guilty of any of these vices, prayerfully repent.

Restitute, that is, check all the things in your possession, if there is anything you acquired through any dubious means or through fornication, return them! If it is difficult to return them because of distance or death, see a Bible believing counsellor. Do not be emotionally influenced - if there is anything you inherited from a dead relative and you are attached to it, break the soul-tie and dispose of the thing immediately.

• **Wage war against the pursuers: Pray fire prayers.**

Ignorance of the right prayers: If you do not know how to pray for prosperity, you may not make it.

- **Check your tithes and offerings**

  Have you defrauded God? Have you been stingy with Him? Change!

- **Stop borrowing: Getting yourself indebted calls in the spirit of poverty.**

- **Invest wisely**

  Find out what God wants you to do, how to go about it and when to start. Don't go beyond your means.

You are going to pray some prayers which I recommend, and I assure you that you will be blessed through them. However, first of all obey the simple rules of repentance, restitution, pardon and faith.

The Lord has promised that He will bless His children and they will become the richest and most highly favoured of all people in the world.

The Bible says: I will not despair, for I have believed to see the goodness of the Lord in the land of the living.

However, you cannot enjoy the prosperity of God as a sinner. You cannot continue in sin and ask God to continue to bless you.

PRAYER POINTS

1. I refuse every spiritual demotion, in the name of Jesus.

2. Every strange fire prepared against my prosperity, be quenched, in the name of Jesus.

3. Every power sending my money to spiritual mortuary, fall down and die, in the name of Jesus.

4. Every power scaring away my prosperity, be paralysed, in the name of Jesus.

5. Every familiar spirit spending my money before I receive it, be bound, in the name of Jesus.

6. Every evil foot, walk out of my life, in the name of Jesus.

7. Every satanic re-arrangement of my prosperity, be dismantled, in the name of Jesus.

8. O Lord, lead me to my own land that flows with milk and honey, in the name of Jesus.

9. Every satanic giant occupying my promised land, fall down and die, in the name of Jesus.

10. Anybody wickedly sitting on my money, I withdraw your peace until you return my money, in the name of Jesus.

11. O Lord, empower me to climb the mountain of prosperity, in the name of Jesus.

12. You strongman of poverty, fall and die with your rags, in Jesus' name.

13. You the spirit of famine and hunger, my life is not your candidate, in the name of Jesus.

14. I remove my name from the book of financial embarrassment, in the name of Jesus.

15. Every power reinforcing poverty in my life, loose your hold, in the name of Jesus.

16. O Lord, make me a reference point of divine prosperity, in the name of Jesus.

17. I receive the anointing of excellence, in the name of Jesus.

18. O Lord, let harvest meet harvest in my life, in the name of Jesus.

19. O Lord, let my harvest overtake the sower, in the name of Jesus.

20. I reject every financial burial, in the name of Jesus.

21. I reject witchcraft burial of my money, in the name of Jesus.

22. Every stolen and satanically transferred virtue from my life, be restored, in the name of Jesus.

23. O Lord, create new and profitable opportunities for me, in the name of Jesus.

3

DEALING WITH POVERTY MAGNETS

It is not important for a person to do what people want him to do or what he personally wants to do. The most important thing in the life of anybody, especially a Christian, is to do what God wants him to do, that is, for the Lord to have His way in his life.

Pray like this:

1. *Whether I like it or not, whether the devil likes it or not, O Lord, have Your own way in my life, in the name of Jesus.*

2. *Every satanic storm working against my life, be silenced forever, in the name of Jesus.*

3. *Every satanic alliance against me, scatter, in the name of Jesus.*

4. *Today, O Lord, I must touch the helm of Your garment, in Jesus' name.*

The purpose of this message is that poverty in your life, hiding under any mask, should be located and buried.

MAGNET

Magnet is a device that draws metals to itself. No matter how hidden, once a magnet runs through the place where a metal is, it finds it out.

When Jesus shall appear in heaven, He shall be a magnet and will pull all the people that are like Him, unto Himself. I pray that anything in your life that will debar you from being magnetised to Jesus on that day should be destroyed in the name of Jesus.

Poverty may be sitting on its own, but the magnet in the life of a person will attract it to him.

The secret behind great deliverance is locating the magnet hiding in people's lives. You may have gone through deliverance programme several times and find that the problem persists. It is because there are some powers hiding in your life that are magnetising the demons of this problem to your life.

I have a friend who was shocked when he attended a baby-naming ceremony. As they were about to serve people food, the baby's father came out with a notebook. He ticked the names of those who gave his wife money when she had the first baby. My friend was fidgeting because he did not remember whether he gave her money then or not. It happened that he did and he was served food. Some people were given only a bottle of soft drink.

I don't know whether the baby's father was joking or not but you would agree with me that to some extent it was poverty that pushed him to turn the naming ceremony into a debt-collecting session. Of course, this planted a seed of poverty into the life of the baby.

A woman who feeds her baby on food bought on credit is planting a seed of poverty into the baby's life. Those who use a rat at the naming ceremony and give a piece of it to the mother to chew and put a piece of it on the tongue of the baby, are planting the seed of poverty into the life of the baby because rat represents poverty in the spirit world.

Unfortunately, there are many people with these magnets in their lives.

POVERTY MAGNETS

Poverty magnets and their manifestations are of different kinds. They include the following.

Spirits of Bondage

Romans 8:15: For ye have not received the spirit of bondage again to fear; but ye have received the Spirit of adoption, whereby we cry, Abba, Father.

Doors of Entry

- Lust of the flesh

- Unrepentant sins

- Parental sins

- Ancestors sins

If the children get born-again, they can be washed of these sins by the blood of Jesus as they go through deliverance.

Manifestation of the Spirit

- Chronic unbelief

- Varieties of addictions

- Habitual sins

- Uncontrollable lust and sexual looseness

- Greed

- Roots of bitterness

- Unforgiving heart

- Captivity to satan

- Fear of death

Pray this prayer point: *I bury every bondage in my life today, in the name of Jesus.*

The Spirit of Double-mindedness

James 1:8: A double minded man is unstable in all his ways.

Doors of Entry

- Lack of faith.

- Lack of Bible knowledge.

- Refusal to accept sound doctrines of the word of God.

- Illicit sexual relationships.

Manifestation of the Spirit

- Lack of assurance of salvation

- Uncertainty in the spirit realm and indecision

- Inability to be victorious over sin.

In 1 Corinthians 9:26, Apostle Paul said: "I therefore so run, not as uncertainly; so fight I, not as one that beateth the air:"

Pray this prayer point: *Every spirit of hopelessness, come out with all your roots, in the name of Jesus.*

Spirit of Fear

2 Tim. 1:7: For God hath not given us the spirit of fear; but of power, and of love, and of a sound mind.

Doors of Entry

- Sin

- Sins of parents and ancestors

- Bad experiences during childhood

- Parental neglect.

Manifestation of the Spirit

- Fearful behaviour.

- Profound anxiety and worry.

- Inability to relate to God as Father.

- Nightmares.

- Heart failure.

- Inordinate fear of death.

- Lack of trust, doubt.

- Torments.

- Mismanagement and investing in wrong things.

The spirit of fear is an old demon which started operating in the life of Adam in the Garden of Eden after he had sinned against God.

Genesis 3:9-12: :And the Lord God called unto Adam, and said unto him, Where art thou? [10]And he said, I heard thy voice in the garden, and I was afraid, because I was naked; and I hid myself. [11]And he said, Who told thee that thou wast naked? Hast thou eaten of the tree, whereof I commanded thee that thou shouldest not eat? [12]And the man said, The woman whom thou gavest to be with me, she gave me of the tree, and I did eat.

Pray this prayer point: *Every spirit of fear, depart from my life, in the name of Jesus.*

The Spirit of Pride

Proverbs 16:18-19: Pride goeth before destruction, and an haughty spirit before a fall. [19]Better it is to be of an humble spirit with the lowly, than to divide the spoil with the proud.

Doors of Entry

- Inheritance.

- Gossip.

- Boasting.

- Envy.

Manifestation of the Spirit

- Snobs.

- Unteachable spirit.

- Rebellion.

- Argumentative nature, contentious spirit.

- Self-righteousness.

- Rejection of God's counsel.

The Spirit of Heaviness

Isaiah 61:3: To appoint unto them that mourn in Zion, to give unto them beauty for ashes, the oil of joy for mourning, the garment of praise for the spirit of heaviness; that they might be called trees of righteousness, the planting of the Lord, that he might be glorified.

This is the lot of Christians but many are going about with depressed hearts, not knowing that it is a magnet for pulling into them wicked things. God cannot be found in this kind of situation.

It is a magnet of poverty. The idea of being happy one or two days of the week and being depressed the other days should be dropped. It magnetises arrows from the enemy.

Doors of Entry

- Tragedy - loss of loved ones or things.

- Sins of parents and ancestors.

Manifestation of the Spirit

- Sadness.

- Despair.

- No urge to praise God.

- Root of bitterness that cannot be pacified.

- Loneliness or wanting to be alone.

- Gluttony.

- Sleeplessness.

- Self-pity.

- Hopelessness.

- Broken heart.

Pray like this: (*Insert your name) reject every spirit of heaviness, in the of Jesus.*

Whatever will hinder the joy of the Lord from being my strength, fall down and die, in the name of Jesus.

Spirit of Infirmity

Luke 13:11: And, behold, there was a woman which had a spirit of infirmity eighteen years, and was bowed together, and could in no wise lift up herself.

Hospitals are helpless when it is the spirit of infirmity that is dealing with a person. No microscope can detect a demon. No injection can chase out a demon; it will even get fertilised by it.

Doors of Entry

- Sin.

- Unhygienic situations.

- Satanic attack.

You don't have to offend anyone nor be wicked to anybody before they are wicked to you. You may be one of those who do not believe in the existence of witches and wizards. You may have to find out in a hard way that they exist; even Europeans now know that they exist. You could be likened to a person who does not believe in the existence of hell until he dies in his sins and finds himself there.

Other Doors of Entry

- Heredity.

- Evil dedication before, during or after birth.

- Insane condition of living.

Manifestation of the Spirit

- Chronic illness or deformity.

- Bent body or spine.

- Chronic cold and asthma.

- Weakness and fainting.

- Disorder in the body.

- Cancer.

- Depression.

Pray this prayer: *(Insert your name) reject the spirit of infirmity, in the name of Jesus.*

Every arrow of infirmity, go back to where you came from, in the name of Jesus.

The Spirit of Jealousy

Numbers 5:14: And the spirit of jealousy come upon him, and he be jealous of his wife, and she be defiled: or if the spirit of jealousy come upon him, and he be jealous of his wife, and she be not defiled...

Doors of Entry

- Sexual defilement.

- Rage or anger.

- Lack of discipline.

- Strife.

- Parents.

Manifestation of the Spirit.

- Hatred.

- Cruelty or murder.

- Competitive spirit.

- Selfishness.

- Causing division.

- Revenge.

The Spirit of Lies

Deformation of the truth or outright untruthfulness, either to cover up or to deceive.

Doors of Entry

- Seeking enjoyable or flattery prophecies.

- Hatred for pointers to wrong doings.

- Sin of parents.

Manifestation of the Spirit

- Compulsive, habitual lies.

- Deception, operating under delusion.

- Flattery and insincere praise.

- Wishing evil while pretending to be friendly.

- Spirit of religion, pretending to be holy, over-spirituality, hypocrisy.

- Excessive talking, idle gossip.

- Slander.

All these hinder God from bombarding people with wealth. You have to deal with them and chase them out.

Perverse Spirit

Isaiah 19:14: The Lord hath mingled a perverse spirit in the midst thereof: and they have caused Egypt to err in every work thereof, as a drunken man staggereth in his vomit.

Doors of Entry

- Following false prophets/priests.

- Idolatry.

- Generational sin.

Manifestation of the Spirit

- Sexual perversion.

- Addiction to pornography.

- Repeated disobedience to God.

- Twisting the Bible to suit one's purpose.

- Ingratitude.

- Filthy mind.

Seducing Spirits

These are powers that lure people into untruth or sin; they work in a subtle way and their victims do not realize their presence until they have fallen into sin.

Doors of Entry

- Consulting false prophets and teachers.

- Worrying about problems.

Manifestation of the Spirit

- Searing of conscience.

- Double-mindedness.

The Spirit of Slumber

These are powers that weaken and render a person useless.

Romans 11:8: (According as it is written, God hath given them the spirit of slumber, eyes that they should not see, and ears that they should not hear;) unto this day.

Doors of Entry

- Spiritual carelessness.

- Neglect by parents.

Manifestation of the Spirit

- Not knowing right from wrong.

- Not loving others.

- Stagnation.

Spirit of the Devourers

These are powers that eat up good things. They waste good things and dismantle any height.

Malachi 3:8, 11: Will a man rob God? Yet ye have robbed me. But ye say, wherein have we robbed thee? In tithes and offerings.

And I will rebuke the devourer for your sakes, and he shall not destroy the fruits of your ground; neither shall your vine cast her fruit before the time in the field, saith the Lord of hosts..."

Doors of Entry

* Disobedience to God.

* Not paying tithe.

Manifestation of the Spirit

* Chronic poverty.

* Financial calamity, natural disaster.

* Inability to save money.

Legion - Unclean Spirits

Multiple bombardment of evil spirits.

Doors of Entry

- Sin.

- Idolatry, occultism.

- Satanic attack.

Manifestation of the Spirit

- Sleeplessness.

- Suicidal tendencies.

- Supernatural strength.

- Enjoying seeing death.

- Sadistic tendencies.

- Hearing of voices.

- Nightmares.

- Self-exhibition.

- Extremists.

Spirit of Idolatry

An idol is anything that takes the place or position of God in a person's life. The spirit of idolatry is responsible for most of the deeply rooted problems of people, especially Africans face. This is due to the idol worship their ancestors engaged in and which some of them still practise today.

Doors of entry

- Worship of false gods.

- Offering sacrifices to idols/false gods.

- Inherited family satanic worship.

Manifestation of the Spirit

- Conscious or unconscious covenants.

- Adultery.

- Prostitution of the soul and the body.

- Love of the world and money - food, glamour.

- Sexual confusion - equating sexual activities with love, sexual abnormality.

- Marriage destruction

The prayer points I will ask you to pray are both curative and preventive. Do not say you are not concerned.

PRAYER POINTS

1. Every gadget of poverty in my life, be roasted by fire, in Jesus' name.

2. Every spirit of pocket with holes in my life, fall down and die, in the name of Jesus.

3. Every witch or wizard sitting on my money, be unseated by fire, in the name of Jesus.

4. I reject every re-arrangement of my life by household wickedness, in the name of Jesus.

5. Let the magnet of prosperity, be deposited in my hands now, in the name of Jesus.

6. Tell the Lord the kind of prosperity you want:

   The one that will dumb-found your enemies.

   The one that will amaze and shock your friends.

   The one that will swallow your poverty for ever.

7. O Lord, let your boldness enter into my life, in the name of Jesus.

8. Every familiar face harassing me in the dream, be defeated, in the name of Jesus.

9. My life will not accept any satanic arrow, in the name of Jesus.

10. I refuse to sit for any satanic examination, in the name of Jesus.

11. I refuse to be spiritually stagnant, in the name of Jesus.

12. Every clever devourer, loose your hold, in the name of Jesus.

13. I don't want small breakthroughs, I want giant breakthroughs, in the name of Jesus.

14. My life will not follow any evil family pattern, in the name of Jesus.

15. I withdraw my progress from every evil altar, in the name of Jesus.

16. Any power paralysing my prayer life, fall down and die, in the name of Jesus.

17. I possess my foreign benefits, in the name of Jesus.

18. Every curse issued against me by satanic prophets, fall down and die, in the name of Jesus.

19. Every mark of poverty upon my life, be rubbed off by the blood of Jesus, in the name of Jesus.

20. Every spirit of leaking pockets, fall down and die, in Jesus' name.

21. Every problem mocking my prayers, fall down and die, in Jesus' name.

22. (Pick from the list) . . . be buried permanently, in the name of Jesus.

    Every stone blocking my progress,

    Every witchcraft decision against my life,

    Every satanic gathering concerning my progress,

    Every "Pharaoh" and "Goliath" harassing my life,

    Every satanic prophet boasting against me,

    Every satanic angel troubling my life,

    Every marriage destruction,

    Every satanic joy concerning my life,

    Every satanic poverty.

23. Thank the Lord for answering your prayers.

4

THE BATTLE AGAINST WASTERS

Proverbs 18:9: He also that is slothful in his work is brother to him that is a great waster.

Isaiah 54:16-17: Behold, I have created the smith that bloweth the coals in the fire, and that bringeth forth an instrument for his work; and I have created the waster to destroy. [17]No weapon that is formed against thee shall prosper; and every tongue that shall rise against thee in judgment thou shalt condemn. This is the heritage of the servants of the Lord, and their righteousness is of me, saith the Lord.

The spirit of wasters is the most terrible demon that has demoted the blackman. It has been doing a lot of havoc all over the world.

WASTE

To waste means to use wrongly, not put to full use, or not used at all. It means to render something useless by damage or to make something worthless. Before it takes over a place, it would have damaged the individuals there.

It grieves my heart to see many people who are not walking according to the time table of God for their lives.

Do you know where your God-given prosperity lies? Many people spend years drawing water, hewing wood and serving their oppressors. Have you identified what will make you prosper? What do you derive joy in doing? What do you enjoy doing for other people? What are the things that God has planted into your life that could be useful to other people? What can you do with minimal assistance? What do you enjoy doing that can benefit others?

If you do not have clear-cut answers to these questions, then, the wasters are already in place. If you do not know how to pray aggressively, you have to learn it because the powers of the wasters must be wasted. Crying or regretting that they are in your life, will not do you any good. It is useless to give up.

Many men are being wasted day after day. In the first place, they have not found out what God's plan for their lives is. So, when the devil wants to finish them up, he makes them go about with strange women.

No one gets younger, you must know what God wants you to do in life now. Don't allow the enemy to decide for you; no matter what your age is, do not allow the devil to dictate the direction of your life.

Many women are being wasted; some of them are in the state they are today because of an accidental pregnancy. They do not love the men who impregnated them. It just happened that they met and before they knew it, they became pregnant and could not get rid of it. Many of them are collapsing under the heavy weight of the yoke of such pregnancy- imposed marriages. They are being wasted away.

The powers of wasters are a strong force. The Lord has invested so much in our land and it is very rich. Anything you plant grows at one season or the other. We have oil and other minerals, and all sorts of blessings.

For example, at a time, there was a particular group of people in England trying to see if they could grow some tropical plants over there. But there is no crop that cannot grow in Nigeria.

Nigeria is a blessed country: blessed with people with intelligence in large number. Nigerians are found everywhere and in every field of endeavour. They excel wherever they go. They are very intelligent and wealthy. But the wasters are at work in the lives of individuals and in the nation. In fact, the wasters are at work all over Africa in diverse forms. The problem is not leadership or lack of planning; the demon to be dealt with is that of wastage.

In Lagos, many years ago there were buses solely for students and pupils at a token fare. As the number of children using them increased, the government provided more buses.

Suddenly, the number of the buses started to decrease and now, school buses are nowhere to be found - they have gone into extinction. These days, you can find students at bus stops at 9a.m., waiting for buses to convey them to school.

Before the spirit of wastage starts work in a nation, it would have succeeded first in the lives of individuals. This is very sad.

THE SPIRIT OF WASTAGE

This is very deceptive

It does not present itself to people the way it is and when it arrives, it blinds people from seeing the secrets and opportunities of success - they are left in obscurity and often deluded.

It is shapeless

It is indescribable but can be felt in its manifestations in the form of failure, impossibility, set-backs, bad-luck, etc.

Many people think they are unlucky in life and resort to dubious or occultic means of solving problems, instead of going into serious praying and fasting and addressing wasters aggressively. There is nothing like luck; a person is either blessed or cursed. It is the spirit of the waster that pumps sicknesses and diseases into the lives of people, so that they will spend all their money seeking treatment and eventually it will take their lives and they would have wasted away without fulfilling their divine destinies.

This spirit sometimes manifests in the form of impatience. It makes people rush into decisions and take drastic steps that make them lose money, possessions, relatives, family and even their own lives. You can find it manifesting in banks, companies, on the highways, in homes, everywhere, even in churches.

A simple example can be found at bus-stops in Lagos. A bus comes and before the driver stops, people start rushing and hustling to get on and in the process, they hit one another, offend one another and quarrel and their journeys become uninteresting. The driver's impatience makes him not reach the bus-stop and people start alighting whilst the vehicle is still in motion.

It is said that *"the patient dog eats the fattest bone."* If you want to move permanently from defeat to victory, from poverty to prosperity, from failure to success, from nobody to somebody, you have to deal with the spirit of the wasters. A person might have millions of naira or dollars in his possession, but if the spirit of the wasters is in his life, the money will be lavished or wrongly invested or devoured like the wealth of the prodigal son (Luke 15:11-16).

The powers of the waters make people give up on trying harder, it doesn't make them see any possible solution to their problems. They make people think aimlessly and go through life without a divine purpose. It is unfortunate that many people go through life expecting only bad things to happen. When the worst eventually happens, they would say that they knew it would happen and that the breakthrough they had was temporary and too good to be true.

Some people blame others for their calamites, instead of dealing with the spirit of the wasters. There is an adage in Yoruba language which says: *"If it takes a person ten years to prepare for madness, when will he go into the market for the full manifestation of his insanity?"*

Pray this prayer point with boiling anger: I reject every manifestation of backwardness, in the name of Jesus.

The spirit of the wasters does not allow people to understand that sometimes God allows them to go through painful experiences so that they can become champions.

A champion is someone who has triumphed over great enemies. David was a champion. There is hardly anyone who can become a champion without fighting, besides, there is no victory without any battle but the powers of the wasters will not allow people to understand this fact.

People are said to be great for God because they have won many battles. It is the fellow who sits for and passes an examination that is promoted. God might be testing you at this moment and it is to make you a champion.

When God tested Belteshazzar, He found him wanting. He said: *"Thou art weighed in the balances of the Almighty and thou art been found wanting (Dan. 5:26-28)."* In a way, God was telling Belteshazzar that he had wasted his life.

In reality, many physical trials that have happened to Christians are spiritual strategies for promotion. An untested product in a factory is unreliable and there is no guarantee for it.

Great spiritual assignments are reserved for people who do not break down under trial. Anyone looking at his problems from beneath will be bugged down under their weight. The one who looks at them from God's angle will see them as an opportunity to record exciting testimonies.

When Peter asked Jesus to ask him to walk on the sea and fixed his focus on Jesus, he (Peter) remained afloat. The moment he looked down and focused on the waves, he began to sink (Matt. 14:22-29).

Many people are wasting their time stoning Moses like the Israelites. When Moses brought them out of Egypt they were confronted by the Red Sea. Looking back, the host of Egypt was after them and they accused Moses of taking them out from Egypt where at least they had good food to eat and houses to live in, even though they were slaves (Exod. 14:9-12). They would have stoned Moses to death, if God had not intervened. But even if they had stoned him to death, it would not have solved their problem because that would not have removed the Red Sea.

How do people "stone Moses"? By blaming people, things and circumstances for their predicament.

Any problem that cannot be changed, can chain the victim. When the powers of the wasters are in operation in the life of a person, he will not fulfil the purpose of God for his life and will go through life aimlessly. He would live a life of spiritual procrastination and spiritual enemies would change his destiny.

Many people are poor because they have spent their money on unprofitable projects that have wasted their investments, time and energy. All leaking pockets are the operations of wasters.

Sometime ago, a woman invested a lot of money on some goods which were said to be in high demand in a country. She did not pray to seek the face of God on the investment. On getting to the country, she found that the goods she bought were not the ones in demand. She was frustrated because she had spent all that she had on them and had got a loan to ship them there.

Many families are being wasted through polygamy, divorce, separation and that is why people go from wife to wife or husband to husband.

A sister came to me one day, and said that she would like to remarry. I asked her who the second man was and she told me he was a widower who just lost a wife for the fifth time. I told her to go and find out what happened to the five women he married and what killed them. The man was under the attack of the wasters.

The Israelites wasted away in the wilderness. If Bartemaeus was not determined, he would have wasted away in his state of blindness (Mark 10:46-52).

Some people are wasting their talents. Some have buried theirs. Some are using theirs to glorify the devil. One of the things that God hates and which can send people to hell is the burying of talents like the unprofitable servant who was thrown into hell (Matt. 25:15-30). Many Christians come to church without being useful with their talents. They only warm benches. The Lord will ask them what they did in His household and they must answer, except they change.

The devil can waste a person's health by getting him a job that will use up his energy, strength and abilities. He is capable of wasting people's blessings, abilities, prosperity and spiritual power. The power of the wasters makes people work hard but get little or nothing in return.

Cain, was a wasted man by his evil deeds (Gen. 4:1-12). Although Samson's birth was announced by an angel, he wasted it by dying with his enemies (Judges 13, 16), Esau too wasted his life. There are many people who are supposed to be on assignment for God but are doing nothing.

You can decide today to put a halt to the activities of the devil. The worst and most pitiable thing in the universe that anyone can do is to waste his or her life.

Before you were born, God knew you and had a purpose for your life. You have to find out what that purpose is, and start working towards fulfilling it, otherwise you may be putting your life in danger. It is better to decide to fulfil the purpose of God for your life.

You may be running a race that nobody asked you to run. You may win that race but God did not plan it for your life. The fact that you are doing something good does not mean that you are doing the right thing. *"A good idea is not necessarily a godly idea."* When the life of a person is not fulfilling God's purpose, it is being wasted.

The Psalmist did not want his life to waste, that was why he prayed some radical and violently hot prayers, using the lightning of the Lord, commanding the ground to swallow his enemies, breaking the teeth of the enemy and dashing them to pieces. He was really violent. You too will use the weapon of prayer to stand against wasters.

We are praying that wealth should change hands. God has set aside an assignment that each of us should carry out. He has designed a map for us. If you do not go by His design and plan, you will not get to the expected destination. Many children of God are roaming the streets because they are not in the Lord; until they turn to the Saviour, they will not make a headway.

Once God has decided that your life should take a particular pattern and you depart from it, you have opened the door to wasters. A lot of pastors, deacons, deaconesses and ushers have departed from the way the Lord marked for their lives. Some who are supposed to be apostles to the nations are still in a gathering where they are distributing biscuits as sacrifice, thinking that they are playing church. Some, whom God have promoted and given an assignment, are busy posing as the sixth or seventh wife of a rich man. God is looking at them with pity, saying He has an assignment for this person, if only she would come to Him.

You need to break loose from the grip of the wasters. Take a look at your life. Have you done anything that is of lasting value for the Lord? He keeps saying: "I spent so many years for you, suffered for you, what have you done for me?" Check your life and see if there is anything that can be pointed at, that you have done For the Lord; whether you are young or old, examine your life.

May be all you have recorded for yourself is being "Chief A" and when you die your children will struggle over your possession, they are of different mothers and are not friendly, one with another; their mothers too will fight it out among themselves. Some pastors have turned themselves into Gehazi. They are running after gifts and money from the congregation and do not have the courage to tell them the blunt truth of the Gospel.

You have only one life to live, there is no reverse journey, it is one-way traffic. It is like an arrow shot. It started somewhere someday and it is going to end somewhere, someday. In God's record, will it be said of you that you spent your life according to the will of God or that you wasted it?

A man of God said there are two ways by which people leave the world: they either die or are killed. Those who die are those who fulfilled God's purpose for their lives. Those who are killed are those who allow one thing or the other to take them away from God's plan for their lives.

In Africa, there are witches in every family, whether extended or nuclear. They eat up the prosperous members by taking their virtues and goodness and then give them incurable sicknesses and diseases.

If you take a close look at children who are always sick or troublesome, you will find out that they are the very intelligent ones. They are the ones that would see snakes and when you get there, you will not see it. This is the handiwork of the wasters. When they kill off the useful intelligent ones in the family, there will be none to help anybody. That is why you find that in some families there are cases of untimely death and those who are alive are very poor.

One of the activities of the wasters in Nigeria is the urge and obsession to leave the country. Hence, you find medical doctors, who graduated from Nigerian universities, in America or Europe doing menial jobs like guards, toilet cleaners, drivers, etc. Some professors are even working under people who would have been their students while they were lecturing at a university in Nigeria. There are many such Nigerians in Saudi-Arabia - all because of money.

The activities of the wasters first started in the lives of individuals. People leave their villages where they were working on farms and come to the cities in search of menial jobs. When they don't get the jobs they expect, they get involved with evil gangs and start taking drugs. Eventually some become armed robbers. The wasters operate in practically every family. I pray that after reading this book they will no longer have a way in your life. It does not matter how far they have gone and for how long they have been there. They must go, in the name of Jesus.

I would like you to pray the next prayer point with all the energy in you: *I refuse to be wasted, in the name of Jesus.*

If God has ordained you to be a millionaire so that you can help others and also propagate the gospel and you are still struggling with how to get three meals a day, then you are a failure as far as God is concerned.

It is a tragedy to be said of you that you used to be hot for the Lord but now you are doing nothing for Him.

It is a pity if you have gone through the university and now you are redundant: you have good certificates but are not doing anything with them. This is the work of the wasters. Similarly, a woman or man who has a family but cannot see the children or the spouse because the other spouse is gone away with a strange woman or man or because of wicked in-laws, is a victim of the wasters.

When you look back and find that you have counted a lot of money in your control in the past, that is, you were rich, but now you cannot point at anything that you have done with your money or when you find that those who are not as qualified as you are or are not as competent as you are in your field, are promoted above you, the wasters are at work.

PRAYER POINTS

1.   O ye wasters of my prosperity, fall down and die, in Jesus' name.

2.   Every aggressor of my comfort, be paralysed, in the name of Jesus.

3.   My blessings shall not stagnate, in the name of Jesus.

4.   I reject weak financial breakthroughs, I claim big financial breakthroughs, in the name of Jesus.

5.   Every hidden devourer, be bound, in the name of Jesus.

6.   I release myself from every evil family pattern of poverty, in the name of Jesus.

7.   I withdraw all my prosperity on any evil altar, in the name of Jesus.

8. You . . . (insert from the list), come out with all your roots, in the name of Jesus.

    - Leaking pocket   - Prosperity paralysis

    - Clever devourer   - Spirit of fragmented life

    - Debt   - Hand shake of poverty

    - Financial paralysis by witchcraft.

9. Tell the Lord the kind of prosperity you want.

10. Today, I must possess my possessions, in the name of Jesus.

11. Every virtue of my life that any enemy is sitting upon, come to me by fire, in the name of Jesus.

12. Anything planted into my life to disgrace me, come out now, in the name of Jesus.

13. Every satanic incense prepared against me, be dissolved by fire, in the name of Jesus.

14. Let the angel that slapped Herod that worms ate him up, go forth now and slap every evil gathering contrary to my life, in Jesus' name.

5

POVERTY MUST DIE

The Bible makes us understand the fact that we can pursue the enemy, overtake him and recover all that he has stolen from us (1Sam. 30:7-8). It is a standing order in the word of God. The Bible is very straight-forward. It gives you the two sides of a coin. It also mentions the fact that curses could pursue and overtake a person (Deut. 28:1-45). So do blessings too.

Note that the spirit of poverty is very stubborn and must be dealt with, with the hammer of the Almighty.

Deut. 28:2: And all these blessings shall come on thee, and overtake thee, if thou shalt hearken unto the voice of the Lord thy God.

Psalm 23:6: Surely goodness and mercy shall follow me all the days of my life: and I will dwell in the house o f the Lord for ever.

When you combine these two scriptures, you will discover amazingly that blessings and goodness are supposed to pursue children of God, contrary to the general belief that they should work very hard to earn a living, hoard the money they make and continue to toil for money.

Here, we can see that those blessings are to pursue and catch up with us. God knows no barrier and no impossibility that is why we are dealing with this theme.

Most of the wealth in our world is in the wrong hands because Christians allowed it. If we stand our ground and disallow some things, it will not happen. Our words are not to be defied because they are by eternal decree by us who are children of the living God by adoption. We were not voted in, so we cannot be voted out. God knows no barrier or impossibility.

Men love supernatural things, they like to see the miraculous and that is why you see people clustering around magicians . The Bible says that signs and wonders shall follow believers. Miracles can pursue and overtake you. The word of God for you is that He has just started His work in your life; He has not finished yet. He is the only true power and fire, He is the only one who has the final say about your life. It is not the doctor, nor the lawyer or the judge that will determine the course of your life.

When God says to your enemy, "Let go," he has no choice than to let you go. God can arise and make a change in your life; you may look around: left, right, forward and backward and find that there is no way out but He is warming up to arise and effect a change in your situation.

As Christians, you should not cheat; even when you are cheated, you should not avenge yourself, He will fight for you. No one can cheat a believer and go scot-free. Haman pursued Mordecai and His wife told him the truth in Esther 6:13:

> And Haman told Zeresh his wife and all his friends everything that had befallen him. Then said his wise men and Zeresh his wife unto him, If Mordecai be of the seed of the Jews, before whom thou hast begun to fall, thou shalt not prevail against him, but shalt surely fall before him.

This is the stand of the Bible concerning the children of God. We must face facts and agree that many Christians are poor and are living below God's standard. That is why the Gospel is spreading at a slow pace. God does not want this situation to be so. He does not want Christians to be poor. Not everybody would be rich but they should live in comfort.

Psalm 34:10: The young lions do lack, and suffer hunger: but they that seek the Lord shall not want any good thing.

Psalm 37:19: They shall not be ashamed in the evil time: and in the days of famine they shall be satisfied.

Psalm 37:25: I have been young, and now am old; yet have I not seen the righteous forsaken, nor his seed begging bread.

WHY POVERTY MUST DIE

Poverty must die because it is not the lot of a child of God.

2Cor. 8:9: For ye know the grace of our Lord Jesus Christ, that, though he was rich, yet for your sakes he became poor that ye through his poverty might be rich.

Proverbs 10:15: The rich man's wealth is his strong city: the destruction of the poor is their poverty.

We have already seen how poverty can kill a person.

Proverbs 20:13: Love not sleep, lest thou come to poverty; open thine eyes, and thou shalt be satisfied with bread.

Poverty could make people avoid a Christian.

If a Christian has to beg and live on others, they will soon start avoiding him; even if he had the word of God to share with them and strength to pray and get people healed and saved.

Poverty make people look down on God.

They would wonder if it is really true that God is the owner of the universe and that He provides the needs of His children.

It is not one of God's promises for God's children. The Bible says it is easier for a camel to pass through the "eye of a needle" than for a rich man to enter into the kingdom of God (Matt. 19:24). But this does not mean that rich men will not get to heaven. It is just that they must not be preoccupied with their wealth or riches, hence, they lose focus on God and eventually miss heaven.

The 'eye of a needle' used to be a small hole at the entrance of Jerusalem. It was left open in the night when the big gate had been locked. Anyone who came in late, passed through the hole and their camels would be made to crawl in through it. If it was laden with heavy loads and the merchants did not want to offload it, they would leave it that way and spend the night outside. Unwanted visitors were also made to sleep outside at night.

People misinterpret this verse. A poor man who is greedy and stingy, is the same as a rich miser.

It makes some people find it difficult to do the will of God.

Anytime Jesus wanted food, He got and ate it. When He wanted to fast, He fasted. He was never hungry because He had no food to eat.

It hinders spiritual growth.

A Christian should read Christian literature written by certain inspired men of God, alongside their Bibles. If a person cannot afford to buy these literature, he misses out on certain things. Even in Bible study, there are some books and commentaries that could enhance Bible knowledge. This does not rule out the fact that a Christian should depend on the Holy Spirit to teach and interpret the Bible to him.

It hinders evangelism.

Many people would like to give towards the spread of the Gospel but cannot afford it. Wealth is in wrong hands and this must be transferred to the hands of the children of God .

Pray this prayer point: I unseat anyone or anything sitting on my money and I render my prosperity too hot for anyone or anything to sit on, in the name of Jesus.

It opens the door to satan in the lives of Christians and the families of Christians.

One day, a couple came to me for the settling of a quarrel between them. As each of them recounted the story, I found out that the root of the problem was poverty.

One of the incidents recounted was that one day as the husband was drinking tea, the wife came in, checked her box of sugar and found that three cubes were missing because she had counted them before leaving. She went close to the man, snatched the cup from him, demanding her sugar. The man claimed that both the woman and the sugar belonged to him, but the woman did not find it funny and a quarrel ensued.

It opens doors to sicknesses and diseases.

If a Christian has money, he will build himself a house the way he wants it; he would not have to share a toilet with co-tenants who are probably promiscuous and are infected with diseases which can be easily transmitted. If a person has enough money, he will eat the right food and what he wants, not just what he can afford.

It makes people fall easily into temptation.

The feeble - minded would think they have no other choice or alternative than to pick the attractive option of sin. A girl could be lured into sexual sins because she thinks she needs money offered by promiscuous men.

CONDITIONS FOR GOD'S BLESSINGS

- Faith - For example, if you are sick, you need to believe that God can heal you.

- Repentance - For you to come to the saving knowledge of the Lord Jesus Christ, you have to know that you are a sinner and must repent.

- Obedience - To always be under God's protection and His will, you have to obey His word.

- Discipline - If you want to live long and enjoy yourself, you have to do everything in moderation and bridle your tongue.

- Holiness - You have to be cleansed and remain clean, to be able to receive God's anointing.

Until you fulfil these conditions, you are likely to keep inviting agents of poverty, such as devourers, cankerworms, sickness, little foxes, death, etc.

The Bible is against flamboyant living. It destroys life. Extravagance is a sin.

Sometime ago, a woman died and when the stock of her possessions was taken, she had 3,200 dresses in her wardrobes and 300 pairs of shoes. She was buried with only one dress and a pair of shoes.

Many sisters write to testify to how the Lord has helped them moderate their dressing in MFM. The Bible is against the love of money (1 Tim. 6:10) and public display of wealth but wants you to be comfortable as a believer. If you are fasting because you have no money or food to eat, then you are not fasting but are on hunger strike.

WHY ARE BELIEVERS POOR?

Your spiritual level and brokenness could be too low for God to entrust wealth into your hands. The Bible says: "Seek ye first the kingdom of God and His righteousness and all other things shall be added unto you (Matt. 6:33). God will not give you what will kill you.

You should get to a stage where your being rich will not make you backslide or sin against God. By this act, many people keep inviting poverty into their lives, thus, they hinder God from blessing them. If you still have little sins in your life, you are likely to hinder God from blessing you. Sins like anger, malice, greed, dishonesty, lying and so on, will hinder Him. Forsake them and surrender your all to Him.

Unrighteousness

Many people are humble because they are poor. Once they become rich, they become puffed up and the liking for sin sets in. They would want to marry more wives , increase their appetite, etc.

In the Psalm we examined earlier David says: "... I have never seen the righteous forsaken..." Many people are serious Christians because they are poor. Once they have money, they become too occupied and busy to come for service . Some women are praying to God for the promotion of their husbands but God knows that if such husbands become rich, they will be going about with strange women and even build houses for them.

Due to poverty, some people have no fans in their rooms. This makes mosquitoes deal with them and they are able to keep awake to pray at night. Once they get a fan or an air-conditioner, they would not keep vigils any more because they can't wake up until 6:a.m.

Many people forget the house of God when they are rich . They used to go to church by bus when they were poor and would even preach in the bus before getting to their destinations. Now that they have cars and a driver, they come late or don't come at all, because the driver comes late. God sees all these.

When business was not booming, some people closed their shops to go to church, but now customers are so many that they cannot leave the shop to come to church. Overtime at work will hinder some people from going to church; they get to work very early but go late to church.

All these people are like Adam who blamed God for the woman He gave him. They are blaming God for giving them jobs and money. God normally withdraws that which stands between Him and men in order to save their souls.

Check your life, beloved. Are you broken enough to be trusted by God and to commit the riches of the Gentiles into your hands? Are your hands clean enough to hold His wealth?

Not giving to God

Proverbs 11:24-25 says: There is that scattereth, and yet increaseth; and there is that witl.holdeth more than is meet, but it tendeth to poverty. The liberal soul shall be made fat: and he that watereth shall be watered also himself.

Luke 6:38 buttresses the point thus:

> Give, and it shall be given unto you; good measure,
> pressed down, and shaken together, and running
> over, shall men give into your bosom. For with the
> same measure that ye mete withal it shall be
> measured to you again.

This is where the enemy has blindfolded many believers.
Many pray hard for prosperity but do not sow seeds. It is like a
student going for an examination without reading or a woman
who wants to get pregnant on her own, without a man. You
have to sow seeds and God will multiply them. Many people
ask how to tithe, they want to know if it is 10 per cent of the
gross or the net pay. It is better to pay more than 10 per cent
than pay less.

Do not treat God like a beggar, giving Him what you do not
need. If it is difficult to give to God when your situation is
difficult, you will not find it easier when you are rich. Sowing in
the time of famine attracts abundant blessings and prosperity.

The woman in Mark 12 gave all she had, even though it was
not much. She was commended by Jesus, as having given
more than the other person who was richer. If you can afford
more than 10 per cent, give it. If you forget to pay your tithe,

you are inviting poverty into your life. If you think your tithe is too huge for God, you are inviting poverty into your life. If you earn ₦20,000 and you find it difficult to tithe ₦2,000 which is 10 per cent, you are inviting poverty into your life.

Wise believers give more than 10 per cent. They challenge God with their seeds. If you do not feel the pinch when you give to God, you have not started. Many people are tight-fisted when it comes to giving towards the Gospel. Giving is a sacrifice and you must feel its effect. King David, a man after God's heart was a sacrificial giver - he would not give to God anything that cost nothing (II Sam. 24:24). Those who borrow tithes are insulting God and are looking for trouble. A single problem can finish your whole money.

The principle of giving makes you experience many financial breakthroughs but fear and unbelief will keep you in poverty. Many Christians do not give towards the work of God. The Bible wants you to give and shows you how to go about it. The money that God needs to finish His work had been in the world before you were born. God will not force you to part with your money. You have to do it yourself and this will open the door of your life to blessings. Many good things will begin to happen to you.

The Bible says when you give to God, you should give unselfishly, that is, in total surrender to God, sacrificially. Your offering is measured by what you have left and not what you give. You should give generously and willingly, cheerfully, systematically and at any opportunity you have (2 Cor. 9:6).

You should give in proportion to your income. Give without grudging, willingly, without complaining. The Bible says you should not allow your left hand know what the right one is doing (Matt. 6:3). Don't wait until you are coaxed by someone to give, so that you can have breakthroughs. You should give willingly and regularly and not with display or open show. If you have not been giving correctly, I want you to start now.

Limiting God

Psalm 78:41: Yea, they turned back and tempted God, and limited the Holy One of Israel.

Many people look down on themselves, they think they are not eligible in certain cases. They limit God in their speech and actions. Many don't believe that anything good can happen to them beyond their salaries or income. Anytime they pray, they focus their attention on what appears to be obvious. They are not on the look-out for the miraculous and the supernatural.

That is why, when you ask some people how they are faring, their answers are negative: "There is no improvement," "well, pray for us," "rough," "just managing," "not too bad." All these negative thoughts invite poverty into the lives of God's people. The Bible says: "With God, nothing shall be impossible (Luke 1:37)."

Matthew 19:26: But Jesus beheld them, and said unto them, With men this is impossible; but with God all things are possible.

In the dictionary you will find the words "impossible" and "difficult" with their meanings but they are not in the word of God.

Wrong business or profession

In Luke 5 you will read the story of Peter as a fisherman. He was toiling and working hard, looking for fish to catch, whereas God ordained him to be a fisher of men to go out and look for men and draw them unto God. God does not bless wrong things. Check prayerfully and know if you are in the right business or profession.

If you are confused, pray the prayer points on "Make Your Way Plain Before Me" (see the last set of prayers before the last chapter, page 177).

Pray them vigorously for about three weeks at a go and the Lord will make you know which direction to take. If you are jobless, face the reality of the situation and place it at the feet of the Lord and He will surely intervene.

If you are doing what God wants you to do and you encounter problems, the Lord will arise and seek you out because He gave you the go ahead in the first place.

Students are not to pick just any course of study. They must know what God wants them to study and at the end, they will get a suitable job.

Many Christians are spiritually lazy and do not wait upon the Lord to seek His face until He does something about their situation. Such people do not receive visions or revelations about the will of God for their lives. They could start praying but end up abandoning it.

The fact that the Lord is not talking to you shows that you need to make some spiritual adjustments. Check if you are doing the right thing and be sure that God's blessings will come.

In the 80's, a teacher who had a Nigeria Certificate in Education (NCE) was fed up with the debts she was incurring every month. Her salary was not sufficient.

One day, she went for a programme and heard of a message which challenged her to ask God what He wanted her to do. The Lord answered, showed her the piece of land at the back of her house and asked her to start planting vegetables there. Before long, her vegetables was in high demand. She continued and was able to build a house from the proceeds.

If God asks you to sell something, even water, and you obey, you will prosper in a way that it would seem that God's blessings are for you alone. Many traders close up in the evening with sadness written all over their faces because there were no sales. Many a times some lament their fate and have no hope of being able to continue.

One day, as I was parking my mini bus, a boy walked up to me and asked if I wanted passengers. I was surprised and said no. I then asked him why he was a bus stop tout and he said that was his means of livelihood, and even the means of feeding his aged parents.

Giving place to the enemy

Ephesians 4:27: Neither give place to the devil.

Giving place to the devil means inviting poverty into one's life. There are spirits of poverty and dreams of poverty. Such dreams include: seeing oneself naked in a dream, being broke, roaming about in a market place, selling and not making profit, or wearing tattered clothes.

Many people have strange personalities living in them and these cause poverty until the people are delivered. Such people could invest a huge amount of money in a business but the business will be a failure. The money is wasted and debts are incurred.

Spirit of poverty

It manifests through:

- Unexplainable loss of money despite careful calculations. The person does not know how he spends his money.

- Poverty-stricken dependant people: Who do not want to fend for themselves and whom one finds difficult to chase away.

- Waste: Having to throw spoiled goods or equipment into the refuse bin. Children losing things and their parents having to replace them; being defrauded, or robbed; fire attacks; lack of birth control (having more children than one can cope with); disappearance of clothes, etc.

- Loss of jobs and opportunities

Check your life and see what is wrong with it and how you can rectify it.

PROGRAMME OF ACTION

- Start thinking and if you find that you have cheated God, ask Him for forgiveness.

- Take a positive stand on what you have to do in the house of God.

- Take a step of faith and sell all that you have stored up, which you do not need.

    I know a lady who sold her jewellery and Jezebelian attachments and bought a Mercedes Benz car with the proceeds.

- Pray poverty-destroying prayers.

Beloved, the Lord has promised and He will surely bring it to pass that poverty must die! Every mountain standing before our prosperity shall crumble, in the name of Jesus.

Some sicknesses are not ordinary. They are ladders of poverty which must be broken. Some illnesses demand special food which people find difficult to cope with.

The Bible says that some situations could make heaven become brass.

PRAYER POINTS

1. Every heaven that has become brass, I command you to break open and give way, in the name of Jesus.

2. Every spirit of poverty, I break your control over my life, in the name of Jesus.

3. O Lord, anoint my eyes to see the hidden riches of the world, in the name of Jesus.

4. O Lord, advertise your prosperity in my life, in the name of Jesus.

5. Let the riches of the ungodly be transferred into my hands, in the name of Jesus.

6. O Lord, let divine blessing bombard my life, in the name of Jesus.

7. O Lord, give me dumbfounding breakthroughs, in the name of Jesus.

8. Every curse working against my destiny, be broken, in Jesus' name.

6

THE ANOINTING OF THE TAIL

A person could find himself in a situation which he knows nothing about. It is unfortunate to find oneself in an unfavourable situation as a result of past mistakes and actions of parents and ancestors; the person is like someone born into ignorance and dies in lack of knowledge.

Many are dying everyday without fulfilling their purpose in life or their calling. They end up at the throne of God and they are accused of not doing what they were meant to do. They will then start giving excuses, that it was due to one thing or the other. If they were good students of the Bible, they would have found out that God does not accept excuses and there is nothing to say.

Deut. 28:13: And the Lord shall make thee the head, and not the tail; and thou shalt be above only, and thou shalt not be beneath; if that thou hearken unto the commandments of the Lord thy God, which I command thee this day, to observe and to do them:

Deut. 28:43-44: The stranger that is within thee shall get up above thee very high; and thou shalt come down very low. [44] He shall lend to thee, and thou shalt not lend to him: he shall be the head, and thou shalt be the tail.

If you do not comply with the will of God for your life, if you are disobedient to His word, the promise in verse 13 will not be yours. You will find verses 43 and 44 being your portion. I pray that it will not be so in the name of Jesus, Amen.

If you link verses 43 and 44, you will find out the following ;

• Head and tail.

• Lender and borrower.

Proverbs 22:7: The rich ruleth over the poor, and the borrower is servant to the lender.

The borrower is always at the tail while the lender is always at the head.. That is why we always pray that: "I shall not borrow to eat."

Isaiah 9:15: The ancient and honourable, he is the head; and the prophet that teacheth lies, he is the tail.

If a prophet teaches lies he will be at the tail end, and those swallowing the lies will also be at the tail end.

The purpose of this message to you, is to carefully search out every trace of poverty and destroy it.

One thing that can make you fear God is this: take some dirty water from a gutter and examine a drop of it under a microscope. You will discover living things that look strange, with different shapes and sizes. They are alive in their own world. The same thing would be discovered if you examine the spittle of a sick person. You will find that these living creatures, if transferred to another person by any means, will do the same harm they have done to the first person.

THE TAIL

This is the backside, last, lowest part of a thing. Some people have been reduced to the tail level. This means that they have been lessened, lowered, debased and reduced; they have always come late and last. For example, if there are 200 forms to be distributed, such a person will be numbered 201, which means that the last form was given to the person immediately before him.

Such people who always score the lowest mark or come last, often cheat so that the examination is cancelled.

A man had been studying a course for eight years and made up his mind that he would make it that particular year. He studied deep but one day in the lecture room, someone whistled as the lecturer came in. The lecturer, a lady, was angry and wanted to know the person who whistled. Nobody owned up and she left, saying that they should all consider themselves as having failed.

It happened the way she said and this man was affected even though he was not guilty.

Some people have open and wicked household enemies.

Sometime ago, a very successful man was confronted by a relative who accused him of not buying him anything each time he travelled abroad, whereas he bought for others. He decreed that the man would never go abroad again in his life. This man thought it was a joke and did not pay any attention to what was said.

Later, he started having difficulties and found that he could not travel abroad for more than 10 years.

It then dawned on him and he started praying. The prayers did not have much fire because he did not know about spiritual warfare. Anyway, he continued to pray and he was able to buy a ticket. At the departure hall of the airport, he expected the flight to be announced after sitting there for hours. As nothing happened, he thought he should ask what was going on. At the counter, he was told that boarding had been announced an hour earlier and that the aircraft was ready to leave.

He ran to the boarding gate and got to the door of the aircraft as it was being closed. He wedged the door with his body and told the crew that he had to go on that flight. He was told that his seat had been taken by another passenger and he said he would die there if they refused to take him along .The pilot was informed and he was taken into the cockpit. He did not mind, as long as he was able to travel.

His stubborn pursuers almost succeeded in hindering him again but thank God for the prayers he had prayed and his consciousness of the fact that he should not allow the enemy to overcome him. Christians' ignorance of the warfare waged against them, makes the enemy to succeed in putting some Christians in the tail region. Today, you must bury the corpses of your poverty, in the name of Jesus.

The Bible shows us that there is a position of head, and another of tail. There are what are referred to as being above and being beneath. These positions are awaiting people that will occupy them. I decided a long time ago that I will not occupy the tail region in life. Since these positions are available, they have to be occupied. That is why the Bible says:

... Iniquity shall wax strong and the love of many shall wax cold (Matt. 24:12).

As a child of God, you should decide that you will not be one of those MANY. If you are born again and filled with the Spirit of God, you must know that God has placed in you certain things to make you great. Some people call them "potentials," I call them "your Moses."

Some people have been spiritually blinded and cannot see these potentials. When you tell them to pursue and overtake the enemy and recover what he had stolen from them, they would tell you that there is nothing that had been stolen from them. You must decide to possess your possession.

Some people have killed the "MOSES" in themselves by themselves. Some sold them out on cheap altars of free, illicit sex. Some lost their "MOSES" in Jericho and are busy looking for them in Jerusalem. Some have their potentials on their head or feet but the enemy is sitting on them. Some, it is in their voice or hands or memory that the potentials are hidden but they cannot see them because the enemy has blinded them and has placed an embargo on them.

The parents of Moses in the Bible would never have known

the good things they knew, if God had not given them Moses. Do you know yourself? Have you studied yourself and asked questions about yourself and your life, to know who and what you are and who and what God wants you to be?

If the spirit of the tail is in operation, people will do what they are not supposed to do, they will run the race they are not supposed to run, fight the fight they are not supposed to fight, and sit for the examination they are not supposed to write. They waste their time and energy doing all these things.

Many people would have prospered in their petty businesses in Nigeria and would have become wealthy, if they had not been diverted to thinking that they needed to go abroad. They are made to believe that there are greener pastures abroad, so, they go and get a passport. They are refused visa several times and they decide to change their names. They get another passport in someone else's name and are still refused visa. They now decide to go through the Sahara Desert or by sea but find themselves caught in a web of drug traffickers, though they are innocent. In fact, they are children of God.

They are imprisoned and deported and have no money on them having lost all they gained from the petty business they were involved in before they got obsessed by the idea of going abroad. They are now back to zero level.

THE HEAD

This comprises the eyes, nose, ears, mouth, tongue, teeth, brain. It contains the 'computer' that runs the activities of the whole body. The position of the head is always the top. If you see anyone walking with his head on the ground and his legs up in the air, you will automatically run away from him, because it is a reversed position.

The head has a weapon called teeth. It can tear anything apart. The Lord says that you shall be the head and not the tail, so the spirit that should be operating in you is that of head and not tail

A cow has a tail, close to it is its anus; with the tail, it chases flies away. You may cut off its tail and it will still remain a cow. There would be no serious consequence if it has no tail, although it may not be able to chase away flies when it has a wound on its ears.

Some people lose their jobs without any serious consequence to the company. They even have nobody to weep for them or to fight for them to regain the job.

It is time for Christians to arise and take up their positions. There are prayers to be prayed that will make you, as a Christian, occupy your rightful position in the society. God is not against His children occupying top positions in the society.

We should actually look for these positions, so that our destiny will not be in the hands of the wrong people.

Before the wealth of the Gentiles can come to you, you have to depart from the tail region . The only way to do this is to cry unto the Lord. He says; "Ask and you shall be given; knock and it shall be opened unto you (Matt. 7:7)."

There are many spirits mentioned in the Bible, Some good and some bad.

Good spirits

Spirits of adoption, counsel, glory, grace, humility, knowledge, meekness, understanding, wisdom.

Bad spirits

Spirit of bondage, error, slumber, anti-Christ, unclean spirit and familiar spirit.

Since these spirits exist, you can find the anointing that goes with them.

For instance, if a person is afflicted by the spirit of slumber, he would have the anointing to sleep under any condition and cannot easily be woken up. Such a person can sleep during prayers and even while on his feet.

There is the spirit of the head and that of the tail. Many people have allowed the spirit of the tail to creep into their lives.

PEOPLE IN THE TAIL COMPARTMENT

They live a floating life and are capable of doing many things at the same time.

They function everywhere without having a stable job, even though they are trained in specific professions.

A dead fish floats and can be carried away by water current. So also, a person living a floating life can be carried away by the tide of life. This is an evidence of being in the tail compartment.

Many people study courses that do not align with their lives. Many medical doctors are now operating poultry farms and some engineers are running hairdressing salons. Similarly, many drivers are repairing bicycles just as there are prophets and prophetesses who sell fish and chicken. The Holy Ghost will just be watching until the person changes.

Those who have determined to remain at

the same level and manage life.

They are people who are following evil family patterns.

They claim that they are like their fathers or mothers and they are not doing anything about it. They think it is normal, even though they are not enjoying it.

Unseriousness in holiness.

The Bible says that "without holiness, no man shall see God" (Heb. 12:14). God cannot use any unclean vessel, so you have to purge yourself of every sin.

Those constantly afflicted with sicknesses and diseases.

They are known to be sick and have come to accept the fact they are sickly and they cannot do certain kinds of work.

Those who are unable to persist in whatever they are doing.

They easily get fed up or attracted to something else whilst doing other things.

Those who are married to wrong and incompatible spouses (they are unequally yoked).

It is only God that can deliver such people because marriage is for ever. We always tell our spinsters and bachelors that they should first know and fulfil the purpose of God for their lives before getting married. The problems many people face today is the fact that they did not seek the face of God before choosing their spouses. Some have been slowed down in their walk with God by their spouses; even the businesses of some are influenced negatively by their spouses.

Polygamy

Some people have inherited polygamy from their parents and ancestors. It runs down the family even if they were female. Some people find themselves leaving one spouse for the other or getting more than one, even if it was not their original plan in life.

Evil companions.

If you befriend God's enemy, you cannot receive His blessings. You cannot bless who God has cursed.

Doing the wrong jobs.

When God is not with you in what you are doing, you will occupy the tail region.

Inability to concentrate in anything.

Bad use of time

When you have the tendency to waste time.

Possession of wealth of sorrow.

Lack of vision.

This is when a person has no ambition or prospects of improvement.

Desire for revenge.

This refers to lack of forgiveness and wanting to pay back offenders in their own coin.

Negative gossip and backbiting.

Whatever your position is, it is more profitable to tune in to the leadership of the Holy Spirit and talk only when He asks you to do so.

Ignorance is another factor.

This is not knowing what to do or how to pray. The devil wants to keep people in his cage by making them remain ignorant and believe wrong doctrines.

A brother was sent to New York to preach. I advised him to preach as if he was in Ajegunle in Nigeria. He did and people started screaming and falling when they were praying . His sermon was entitled "Breaking the Evil Cage." Many of those he preached understood the message and prayed to breakthroughs.

A long time ago, a man cried unto God that he wanted to be rich. God ministered to him to open his Bible that his prosperity was in it. He did and found a 20 dollar note in it . He did not understand what God meant - that his prosperity would be in the preaching of the Gospel. He did not do so because he did not understand, and he died almost as a pauper.

Poverty-destroying prayers cause confusion in the camp of the enemy. The devil knows that if he sits on the wealth of Christians, they would not grow spiritually and the work of God would not grow. God is ready to give His children His prosperity if they are ready to receive it.

Unbelievers do not have the right to ride new cars while the children of God are unable to buy even a fairly used car. It is written of Christians, "Thou shalt tread upon serpents and scorpions and nothing shall by any means hurt you (Luke 10:19)," and "The earth is the Lord's and the fulness thereof (Ps. 24:1)." Christians should reject poverty and hate it with perfect hatred.

The spirit of debt is another factor.

Some people borrow everything. They buy things on credit, even those things that are not essential or that they don't need. Make up your mind never to go into borrowing or buying anything on credit, so that the spirit of debt will not creep into your life.

Make do with what you have until you pray yourself into prosperity. Don't buy what you don't need. Owing brings in the spirit of poverty. When you owe and you are unable to pay back, you are incurring curses upon your life because the person you owe is not taking it lightly with you.

Lying or negative modification of the truth.

You should be able to say "Yes or No" at anytime. Don't talk about people, if you cannot repeat what you said before them. There is no small lie, no diplomatic lie: every untruthfulness is sin. Jesus said: "Ye are of your father the devil and the lusts of your father, ye will do; he was a liar from the beginning, therefore, he is a father of lies (John 8:44)." Anybody who tells lies is a child of the devil masquerading as a Christian.

Being critical of others.

If you want everything to be spotlessly correct, it is good but you should give recognition to the frailties of others. Don't condemn them for their mistakes, but correct them in love. Rather than pose as lord, bring people up to perfection in love.

Jesus walked and worked with the most inadequate and uneducated people and He brought them up in the way of the Lord, to do His work .Do not criticise with the aim of destroying others.

Greed

Those who go into business with people and refuse to give them their rightful share.

Procrastination

Those who refuse to do what the Lord wants them to do at the time He wants them to do it, despite warnings and directives.

Talkativeness

Some people talk themselves out of their anointing and expose themselves to their enemies .There are some things you do not discuss with just anybody until it comes to full manifestation.

Lack of knowledge of the word of God.

If you are lazy in reading the Bible, you will not know what God says about your situation in His word and you will not know the weapons of warfare that He has put at your disposal against the enemy.

Many people don't want to be in the tail region. In fact, they know what God says about them but have been relegated by some powers and they are where they are by compulsion.

Pray like this: *Every battle in the heavenlies against my prosperity, be paralysed now, in the name of Jesus.*

POWERS THAT FORCE PEOPLE TO
THE TAIL REGION

Household wickedness

Those who sold Joseph into slavery were of his family,

precisely his brothers (Gen. 37). Household wickedness has limited the progress of many people and they do it in many ways. Sometimes it is done through sicknesses that siphon money. The drugs for certain sicknesses are very expensive.

While I was at the University of Reading, one of my classmates almost died of malaria. He came home on holidays and when he got back to England, he took ill. The English doctors tried their best treating him for all sorts of sickness to no avail. All his money went on this treatment. We, Nigerian students, formed a team, approached the doctors and tried to convince them that the boy had malaria and that we had the cure . They vehemently refused to release him to us, saying they had to seek permission from the Academy of Public Medicine. We threatened to set the hospital ablaze before they allowed us to give him Chloroquine and he got well.

This could have been seen as ordinary malaria but it was an arrow fired at him from home to ruin his finances and he would have died eventually. We dealt with the situation with prayers and boldness and he was delivered .

Forces of household wickedness could sponsor dismissal from a promising job. Many would table case at their witchcraft meeting and they would carry out their evil decision through their agent at the person's place of work.

They could put a mark of hatred and rejection on people and they will not be appreciated or loved, wherever they go. There is a Chinese proverb that says : "God save me from my friends and I will deal with my enemies." This means that those whom you see as friends or relatives could be the authors of your problems.

Unprofitable friends

Anyone who wants to pass an examination should move with those who have once sat for it and passed, not those who failed. If you move with failures and faithless people, it means you are planning to fail. If your friends are discouraged and fed up with life, they will have nothing good to offer you.

Proverbs 13:20: He that walketh with wise men shall be wise: but a companion of fools shall be destroyed.

If your friends are discouraged, worried and prayerless, you will become like them. Similarly, If they are prayer-warriors, they will gear you up to become one.

The secret of the success of Joshua lay in the fact that he moved close to Moses, he sneaked in when Moses was with God and tapped some of the anointing which helped him later in life. If your friends are unbelievers, you will be dragged to the tail region by the forces that are working against them.

The emptiers

They hinder people from working hard; they allow them to go about and gather wealth and then waste it. Some sisters married poor men, worked hard and helped their husbands become rich and notable.

Suddenly, these men started having affairs with strange women who became their second and third wives and had children for them. At the end of the day, the wife of their youth was forced out of the matrimonial home and some of them even died in the hands of the strange women who wanted these husbands at all cost and by all means. These powers "change the heads" of people and transfer their goodness.

Many girls have lost their virtues and goodness through sexual relationships with men. Many rich men today got their wealth through sexual relationships with girls or women with potentials.

There are a lot of materials in the market, through which these emptiers operate: hair and nail attachments, jewellery, etc. I know some people whose prosperity was stolen through rings, "holy" soaps and sponges, body cream or lotion and perfumes. If you have ever allowed any of these things to be used on you, it is likely that the emptiers are at work in your life.

Curses

This refers to evil words spoken by people. Any time any negative pronouncement is made on or about you or anything that concerns you, you should not take it lightly at all. You should reject it immediately and cancel it in the name of Jesus. If you think it will sound insulting when you say it to the hearing of the person who made the negative pronouncement, because he was joking, then reject it silently and pray in your heart to nullify it.

Some time ago, a white man came to Nigeria for a programme. He was 39 years old and not married. Another man of God asked if he wanted to remain single all his life and he rejected it in the name of Jesus, with all due respect. The other man was surprised at this man. One who makes a negative pronouncement could be a "Balaam " hired to curse you, so reject it.

One day, a Christian sister who was pregnant was accosted by a white garment prophet who said if she did not make a sacrifice she would die at child birth. She grabbed the man's garment and ruffled him until people gathered. She insisted that he revoked what he said in the name of Jesus. The people who gathered also asked him to revoke it and he did.

You could devote a whole day to praying to revoke curses. If you keep silent concerning pronouncement made jokingly or unconsciously, it means that you accept them.

Some government workers die poor because of the curses they incurred as they were carrying out their duties. Such curses stay if you are prayerless. Some parents issue curses on their children while rebuking them, such pronouncements become binding.

Disobedience

Any form of disobedience to God and man makes you vulnerable to these evil powers.

Laziness

Physical and spiritual laziness are bad. They encourage these powers to keep a person in the tail region and put him in trouble. If a Christian is slack in matters concerning God, he will be slack in every other thing and this drives away progress. Laziness has turned some girls into prostitutes. You are going to pray some prayers in this section and I want you to believe God for miracles. As far as God is concerned, you can reap from where you sowed and also from where you did not sow because: "The earth is the Lord's and the fulness thereof (Psalm 24:1)."

The correct order of things is for unbelievers to see us, wonder and desire to be like us, and ask us to take them to our God. The case should not be the reverse where Christians are seen begging and depending on unbelieving relatives. There must be a reverse now!

In an aircraft, there are three categories of seats and compartments. Those in the first class are treated like kings, they are spoiled with care. Those in the business class are treated with respect too. Those in the economy class struggle to get in, beg the aircraft crew for special services and eat common food. Christians are to be first class citizens anywhere.

PRAYER POINTS

1. All my buried virtues, be released to me now by fire, in Jesus' name.

2. Angels of the living God, prepare special fire and burn away every poverty, in the name of Jesus.

3. Every invitation to the arena of poverty in my family , die, in the name of Jesus.

4. Every geographical hindrance to my breakthroughs, clear away, in the name of Jesus.

5. Today, I shall bury the corpse of m y poverty, in name of Jesus.

6. I decree a recovery of all my stolen wealth, in the name of Jesus.

7. I command my personal Goliath to fall down and die, in Jesus' name.

7

WEALTH MUST CHANGE HANDS

I pray that your God shall answer and fight for you by fire as you read this chapter.

Pray like this :

- *Every Goliath boasting against me, fall down and die, in Jesus' name.*

- *Every authority hindering the move of God in my life, I challenge you by fire, in the name of Jesus.*

- *Every evil tree working against me, dry up from the roots, in the name of Jesus.*

As you are reading this message, you have enlisted in the group of people that will become rich and wealthy, the group of people who will be catapulted into promotion. Those who have been objects of ridicule shall become subjects of testimony, in the name of Jesus.

The Lord has promised Christians breakthroughs which, however, are not for display in the world, but for us to become His treasuries. That rainfall of breakthroughs is starting right now.

Pray like this: O Lord, I claim my share of the good things that You have deposited in this country, in the name of Jesus.

Deut. 8:18: But thou shalt remember the Lord thy God: for it is he that giveth thee power to get wealth, that he may establish his covenant which he sware unto th y fathers, as it is this day.

God is a wealth-giver, impliedly, He is the genuine source of genuine wealth.

Psalm 34:10: The young lions do lack, and suffer hunger: but they that seek the Lord shall not want any good thing.

Proverbs 8:18: Riches and honour are with me; yea, durable riches and righteousness.

It should be clear to you, that God is not a God of poverty. Since He is our Father, we, His children should not be poor. Today, we have to behave like the lepers who found their way to Syria and found food there. In 2 Kings 7:9, the lepers said: "We do not well if we keep silent . . . We shall suffer if we do."

In the same token, if we keep silent, we would allow the enemy's unrestrained manifestations. If you keep quiet and think you cannot pray about this kind of thing saying that it is carnal to pray about wealth, the enemy will oppress you.

Many believers have no houses of theirs, they are seeking accommodation and the agents will ask for rent for two or three years. Often times, they are unable to cope with such demand. If you complain or remind them of the rent edict, they would ask you to go to the governor to give you accommodation. Therefore, you are obliged to pay.

Wealth is presently in wrong hands. As you are reading this message, if you have ever been referred to, as "poor" (even by those who are obviously very poor and are more on the seamy side of life), I can assure you that it is time for the manifestation of your breakthroughs.

Perhaps your labour has been for Pharaoh and you are continually being oppressed, you are working hard and not getting money for it, you may have been paying your tithe to oppressors, like the Israelites in Egypt, struggling with the strugglers and wrestling with the wrestlers.

Beloved, there is a spiritual force behind money. Unfortunately, unbelievers seem to understand this better than Christians. A man went to a herbalist for money-generating charms. The herbalist told him that there are seven options:

- You should keep a corpse in a cupboard and at the call of the name of the deceased, money will pour down. This would make you rich for a span of two years. The man rejected this.

- You should spend 301 days in a graveyard on the tomb of a deceased rich man. You should not have your bath but can eat and drink there. He rejected this.

- You will be very rich but all your children and wife will die and when you die, you will be buried by strangers.

- You will swallow a small serpent and anytime you need money, you will chant some incantations, vomit the serpent and the serpent will vomit money. This would last for three years.

- You will be initiated into 16 cults and every three years, you will sacrifice an albino.

- You will impregnate three mad women and steal their babies which will be used in making charms. And you should not see the sea; if you do, you will die.

- You will identify three women who are gold-mines but are not aware of it, women who have the virtues to make money and prosper. You will commit adultery with them and their virtues will be transferred to you.

People who accept to do any of these have given themselves up to the devil. They know the spiritual force behind money and recognise its power. They understand this more than Christians do though Christians have cleaner, better and peaceful heavenly method or way of getting money. If we keep quiet, nothing comes. The Bible says: "He that asks receives (Matt. 7:8)." The lepers in the text we mentioned earlier took action and were saved.

If you look at a ₦50 note or any other one, you will find that it represents human blood and toil. It is frightening to note that money can serve or destroy man. It is only God that knows the number of hands that have touched a note and the amount of transactions it has been used to carry out since the moment it was printed at the mint.

Besides, money could be stained with sweat and blood. It is heavy with the weight of human toil. It is possible that people have fought over it or even killed themselves just to possess it. Only God knows what it has done, how many hands have touched it in the course of its silent trip from person to person

- sellers, buyers, the places it has been to, from market to market. It could have bought a wedding ring for somebody or paid for a baptismal card for a person, fed a growing baby, or clothed people.

On the other hand, that money could have bought the stamp on a letter sent to somebody to break his or her engagement to another. It could have paid for the death of a child in his mother's womb through abortion. It could have paid for alcohol which makes a person drunk or produced films that are indecent to watch . It could have hired the body of a woman for a few hours or bought weapons of crime for a person.

Christians make the mistake of not praying on their money. People just collect money and put it in their bags or wallets, on the table or anywhere, without first praying on it. The money could have been taken to the bank by someone who got it through dubious transactions or even bloody deals. You should sanctify any money you receive from anyone before keeping or spending it.

Some people exchange money to introduce poverty into the lives of others. The Bible makes a description of mammon in Luke 16:13:

No servant can serve two masters: for either he will hate the one, and love the other; or else he will hold to the one, and despise the other. Ye cannot serve God and mammon.

In this passage, mammon is personified and treated as an idol, a god. The word "cannot" there, means impossible, you are not able to do so. A person may work for two masters but can only effectively serve one. That is, you cannot carry the tree on both shoulders.

Mammon is the demon power which controls money. It is the devil's salesman. It is the one selling the charms that witchcraft powers and familiar spirits are making use of. It is the one responsible for the distribution of poverty to the human race. It specially attacks Christians. It knows that any Christian in business is involved in spiritual warfare; that is, part of anything he makes as profit goes as tithe and offering into the work of God which depopulates the kingdom of darkness.

The devil likes a situation where Christians are poor and cannot finance their programmes. This demon called mammon, controls other demons like greed, selfishness, poverty and so on. It is now time to defeat that demon and his cohorts. It grips men and enslaves them. This is a very serious matter. As the Bible says, you cannot serve God and mammon. Until you deal with this mammon, you may not get certain things which you are supposed to get.

How to deal with mammon

- Pray on your money.

- Curse the mammon.

- Live a life of holiness.

God is not poor. The Bible says: "The earth is the Lord's and the fulness thereof (Ps. 24:1)." Therefore, God's children should not be poor. Our God is the God of Abraham, Isaac and Israel.

Say this: I know that I am going to prosper.

All the money in the world belongs to God, our heavenly Father. To Him, what you see physically as bank notes, are just like papers; He knows how to transfer wealth to His children.

If God is your heavenly Father, you should know that He will not allow you or any of His children, to go hungry, naked or sick. He is not against His children having money but He does not want the money to have His children.

Money is neither good nor bad. A good man's money does good things. A bad man's money does bad things. If a person cannot control money in accordance with the will of God, it could kill him and send him to hell fire. Be warned!

Wealth must change hands, riches must change hands. Christians must take charge of the wealth of the nations. The Bible says that the sinners are laying up their riches for us to take over (Eccl. 2:26). It is the will of God to give us the riches of the Gentiles. You may be wondering if what you are reading is scriptural. In Exodus 3:22, the Bible says:

But every woman shall borrow of her neighbour, and of her that sojourneth in her house, jewels of silver, and jewels of gold, and raiment: and ye shall put them upon your sons, and upon your daughters; and ye shall spoil the Egyptians.

This was the instruction God gave to the Israelites as they were about to leave Egypt; they left with the wealth of the Egyptians. Would you do the same to your Egyptians? You may say it was not good of them to have done so, but it is not true. The Israelites actually worked hard for the wealth that the Egyptians amassed. They worked very hard and the Egyptians dealt with them very cruelly, that it took the Redeemer Himself to get them out of their bondage. The Scriptures below confirm that God is interested in making His children wealthy and comfortable

Joshua 22:8: And he spake unto them, saying, Return with much riches unto your tents, and with very much cattle, with silver, and with gold, and with brass, and with iron, and with very much raiment: divide the spoil of your enemies with your brethren.

2 Kings 7:1-7: Then Elisha said, Hear ye the word of the Lord; Thus saith the Lord, Tomorrow about this time shall a measure of fine flour be sold for a shekel, and two measures of barley for a shekel, in the gate of Samaria. ²Then a lord on whose hand the king leaned answered the man of God, and said, Behold, if the Lord would make windows in heaven, might this thing be? And he said, Behold, thou shalt see it with thine eyes, but shalt not eat thereof. ³And there were four leprous men at the entering in of the gate: and they said one to another, Why sit we here until we die? ⁴If we say, We will enter into the city, then the famine is in the city, and we shall die there: and if we sit still here, we die also. Now therefore come, and let us fall unto the host of the Syrians: if they save us alive, we shall live; and if they kill us, we shall but die. ⁵And they rose up in the twilight, to go unto the camp of the Syrians: and when they were come to the uttermost part of the camp of Syria, behold, there was no man there. ⁶For the Lord had made the host of the Syrians to hear a noise of chariots, and a noise of horses, even the noise of a great host: and they said

one to another, Lo, the king of Israel hath hired against us the kings of the Hittites, and the kings of the Egyptians, to come upon us. [7]Wherefore they arose and fled in the twilight, and left their tents, and their horses, and their asses, even the camp as it was, and fled for their life.

Beloved, here the Syrians heard noises that made them flee their camp and left all that they had. At the same time the four leprous men felt they could take a risk of going close to this camp. They were hungry and thought they would die in any case. When they got there, they found that there was nobody to challenge them. Then, they went into Samaria to tell the king. This was how the prophecy of abundance in verse one came to pass in a land where there was famine.

The sinners are laying up their riches for us to take over and there shall be transfer, even today, in the name of Jesus.

Proverbs 13:22: A good man leaveth an inheritance to his children's children: and the wealth of the sinner is laid up for the just.

There is no point singing: "My sorrows shall be over when I get home."

It is wrong to think your sorrows will be over only when you die.

Luke 18:28-30: Then Peter said, Lo, we have left all, and followed thee. [29]And he said unto them, Verily I say unto you, There is no man that hath left house, or parents, or brethren, or wife, or children, for the kingdom of God's sake, [30]Who shall not receive manifold more in this present time, and in the world to come life everlasting.

I want you to declare to yourself that the Lord shall effect a change in your life today. The wealth of the nations are in wrong hands that is why you find the children of God suffering. When their children are ill, they have no money to take care of them. They search everywhere in the house and there is no money. They cannot afford to put mosquito nets on their windows neither can they afford to buy insecticide to deal with mosquitoes. So they are bound to fall ill and have malaria. They cannot lock up the windows because they have no fan and the weather is extremely hot. They manage to gather used mosquito repellent from the dustbin or orange peels and they light them in the room. The room is engulfed in smoke which is meant to kill mosquitoes but they in turn get asthma in addition to the malaria inflicted on them by the blood-sucking demon of malaria.

Some of these people go to incompetent medical practitioners instead of qualified medical doctors. Some patients are detained in hospitals for lack of payment of hospital bills.

One day, a man was holding his tummy, rolling on the ground and crying. A kind person approached him and took him to a hospital. As the doctor was preparing the injection solution, the man said he wanted food. The doctor asked if he had eaten that morning; he said his last meal was in the morning of the previous day. He was given food and he asked for more. By the time he finished, the tummy ache had gone.

Proverbs 10 :15: The rich man's wealth is his strong city: the destruction of the poor is their poverty.

God did not ordain man for poverty at all. It is a complete misconception for someone to have such forethought.

When I was teaching in a mixed secondary school, there were always cases of girls put in the family way by unscrupulous men and boys. When the parents were summoned, I noticed that they were poor people, putting on tattered clothes. Their daughters fell into the snare of the devil because of money. I also noticed that the rich people brought their children to school in chauffeurdriven cars. Their children cannot mess themselves up but they themselves go about and mess up other people's children.

A poor man who has a wife selling food, goes there and sees another man patting the backside of his wife. He is unable to say anything because the other man is rich and could be angry and say he would no longer patronise his wife, and other customers too might go with him.

As a laboratory research worker, whenever there was an outbreak of an infectious disease or any deadly one like cholera, we went there and I found that most of the time, the affected places were poverty-stricken.

Beloved, the truth is this: when God created this country, He deposited enough goodness here for His children to enjoy, knowing fully well that there would spring up great evangelists and missionaries who will propagate the Gospel. I want you to take this prayer point with all your might: *Every spirit creating scarcity for me in the midst of plenty, fall down and die, in the name of Jesus.*

When wealth is in the wrong hands, it makes the ordinary man do bizarre things. A woman went to the hospital and was delivered of her baby. She was unable to pay the bills and was detained.

One day, she put the baby in a plastic bag and told the nurse that she wanted to buy something down the road. The unsuspecting nurse allowed her to go and she escaped with her baby.

She laid a foundation of debt for her child by this act. The child became a debtor and lived a life of poverty until he came across a serious deliverance ministry.

Beloved, everyone pays tithe to someone or something . Many years ago, I forgot to pay my tithe in a particular month. One day I drove my mini bus to a petrol station and the young man there, deceived me. He did not put a drop of fuel in the tank but I paid him.

After driving on for a while, the vehicle stopped and a mechanic detected that the fuel tank was dry. I wondered why the young man at the station did that to me and how on earth he could have succeeded. I searched my life for any known sin and found out that I had not paid the tithe I owed God; so, the devourer came in. I quickly paid my tithe.

When God wants to do something in your life, you have to cooperate with Him. There is no point disobeying God and consoling yourself by singing: "This world is not my own, I am just passing through."

Pray this acidic prayer point aggressively: *I refuse to be comfortable with poverty, in the name of Jesus.*

By the time you have dealt with the spirit of poverty, men will rush their money to you because WEALTH MUST CHANGE HANDS.

STEPS FOR TAKING OVER THE WEALTH THAT BELONGS TO THE CHILDREN OF GOD.

Unashamed holiness:

Romans 12:1: I beseech you therefore, brethren, by the mercies of God, that ye present your bodies a living sacrifice, holy, acceptable unto God, which is your reasonable service.

When you surrender your life to Christ, He will entrust wealth into your hands.

If an unholy man handles wealth, it will kill him. You have to be very careful and must live the kind of life God wants you to live. Your attitude to money as a Christian is very important. Money must not rule your life. You should not be like those people who have exaggerated the importance of money and it controls their lives. Once you live a holy and broken life ,God will entrust His wealth and durable, unending riches into your hands.

When the Bible says "durable riches," it means there are some riches that are not durable - they do not last. There is no way a holy person will suffer lack. If he is at the verge of lack his God shall arise.

Have the right type of money: Many people are suffering because they have unlawful money in their possession. Sometimes, when people amass this kind of wealth, they go and gather concubines and strange women as wives. They donate lavishly at bazaars and some priests are unable to correct them because they have already collected precious or valuable gifts from them.

At the end of the day, their lives become worthless. They live at the mercy of doctors and drugs. They are warned not to eat one thing or the other to stay alive. Sometimes, they cannot sleep. They have guards and their windows are secured with iron bars but they cannot sleep in peace. They keep sleepless nights which make them fall sick eventually, and become hysterical.

The Bible says: "The prosperity of fools shall destroy them." That will not be your lot, in the name of Jesus.

Riches without God are a disaster. If you have more money than you can spend, you should use it to help others who do not have; otherwise, you will die and the money will be shared by others.

If you are not born-again and you are not ready to live a holy life, you should not pray for God's wealth; it will destroy you.

Satan took over the wealth of the world from Adam. Today, we have Jesus who shed His blood on the Cross of Calvary and has redeemed us and given us back our wealth.

John Rocky Feller became rich at the age of 33. He worked very hard and got his first million at this age. He concentrated on his business and at the age of 43, he made his first billion. At 53 he became the world's richest man on earth. He was stingy and wicked and was hated by all. He developed all sorts of illnesses and his doctor asked him to prepare his will.

At the news of his eminent death, he started making donations to institutions of research and through that, penicillin was discovered. He gave scholarships and had different foundations which catered for people.

One day in a Christian orphanage, the children had no food to eat but the matron asked them to put their empty plates before them and begin to praise God. They did and as they were rounding off their prayers, there was a knock at the door and a cheque was handed over to the matron, from Rocky Feller. This gave the children the opportunity of having food to eat for a long time.

One day, they decided to pay him a visit and wrote him a beautiful letter. At the gates the guards did not allow them to go in but when Rocky Feller heard it , as sick as he was , he asked the guards to allow them in . When he saw them, he was moved by their love and happiness. From that moment, he began to get better and eventually lived up to the age of 98.

You must have the right attitude to money. God sees your heart and knows your plans. He knows if your aim in getting wealth is for selfish ends. Note the following:

Hate poverty with perfect hatred.

Work hard: Be diligent, don't be a lazy Christian.

The following scriptures enjoin Christians to be hardworking:

Proverbs 22:29: Seest thou a man diligent in his business? he shall stand before kings; he shall not stand before mean men.

Proverbs 24:33-34: Yet a little sleep, a little slumber, a little folding of the hands to sleep: So shall thy poverty come as one that travelleth; and thy want as an armed man.

Proverbs 12:11: He that tilleth his land shall be satisfied with bread: but he that followeth vain persons is void of understanding.

Change your offering and change your destiny.

Sometime ago, a woman took her son to a crusade ground. This boy had about 26 medically diagnosed problems. He had no hands or legs, nor could he talk, etc. The crusade lasted three days and the woman kept going. She gave offering too.

At the close of the programme the evangelist asked the congregation to give an offering towards the spread of the Gospel. The woman had only $20 which would pay her transport home. She jumped out and dropped it in the offering box. It looked crazy.

But towards the end of the service, a word of knowledge came from the evangelist concerning a surgical operation being carried out on a boy who had 26 problems. The woman claimed it and started rejoicing. Immediately, her son jumped up, walking and swinging his hands and shouted: "Mama" for the first time in his life. There were 15 crippled people on wheel chairs in front who got up at the same time. Some people who were on stretchers got up too and started praising the Lord.

As the woman gave her testimony, people got up from all sides of the crusade ground and started giving her money. She went home with more than what she gave to the Lord.

If you are stingy with God, He will not be able to trust you with the wealth of the Gentiles.

Pay your tithe faithfully so that you will not open the doors of your life to devourers who will move in and do havoc.

Some people see some amounts of money as being too big to pay as tithe. It means they are not qualified to get the blessings 10 per cent of which they consider as too big.

Decide to invest your wealth in the kingdom of God.

Pray poverty-destroying prayers.

Pray wealth-releasing prayers.

Poverty - destroying prayers

- I release myself from every spirit of poverty, in the name of Jesus.

- I release myself from wearing the rag of poverty, in the name of Jesus.

- I curse the spirit of poverty to die, in the name of Jesus.

- I release myself from the bondage of poverty, in the name of Jesus.

Wealth -releasing prayers

- O Lord, let the riches of the Gentiles come to me, in the name of Jesus.

- O Lord, let your divine magnet of prosperity be planted in my hands, in the name of Jesus.

- I recover my purse from the hands of Judas, in the name of Jesus.

- O Lord, let there be a reverse transfer of my satanically transferred wealth, in the name of Jesus.

- I recover the steering wheel of my wealth from the hands of evil drivers, in the name of Jesus.

- I refuse to lock the door of blessings against myself, in Jesus' name.

- O Lord, send your angels to bring me blessings, in the name of Jesus.

- Every power sitting on my wealth, fall down and die, in Jesus' name.

- O Lord, transfer the wealth of Laban to my Jacob, in the name of Jesus.

If you have not been paying your tithe, I want you to ask God to forgive you, and promise Him that you will change, in the name of Jesus.

Pray like this: *I release myself from every spirit of poverty, in the name of Jesus.*

A lot of black men are under the bondage of poverty. Most of the poorest nations in the world are in Africa. Pray like this: *Every curse of poverty upon my life, be broken, in the name of Jesus.*

Inherited poverty

Many people work hard and make money but they don't know how the money finishes without their doing anything tangible with it. They then go back to where they started.

Pray like this: *I vomit every spirit of inherited poverty, in Jesus' name.*

8

PRAYER WARFARE

BUSINESS SUCCESS AND VICTORY OVER FINANCIAL DEVOURERS

Confession: Psalms 56:9; 32:8; 23:1,6 Exodus 23:20

1. Let all my enemies turn back because God is for me, in Jesus' name.

2. As they are turning back, let the doors of business opportunities open for me in the morning, afternoon and evening, in Jesus' name.

3. Let profitable business meet me on the way, in Jesus' name.

4. No devourer shall destroy the fruit of my labour, in Jesus' name.

5. You devourers and wasters of fortune, I command you to depart from my life, in the name of Jesus.

6. I use the blood of Jesus Christ to wash my hands and my entire body and make them clear. today.

7. I retrieve my blessings from every evil attack, in Jesus' name.

8. I break every curse of failure, in the name of Jesus.

9. Let the Lord reveal to me every secret behind my problem, in the name of Jesus.

10. I command the devil to take off his legs from any money that belongs to me, in the name of Jesus.

11. Let the ministering spirits (God's angels) go forth and bring in blessings unto me, in the name of Jesus.

12. Let the rod of iron fall on any strange money passed to me, in Jesus' name.

RELEASE OF PROSPERITY ON BUSINESS AND BUSINESS TRANSACTIONS

Confession: Deut. 3:19; 31:66, Psalm 46:1,5; 68:19; 35:27b; 24:1 Jer. 32:27, Phil. 4:19, III John 2, I Sam. 30:8, Job 22:28, Matt. 7:7.

Confess this modified version of Psalm 23.

The Lord is my banker; I shall not owe. He maketh me to lie down in green pastures; He restoreth my loss: He leadeth me beside still waters. Yea, though I walk in the valley of the shadow of debt, I will fear no evil, for thou art with me; thy silver and thy gold, they rescue me. Thou preparest a way for me in the presence of business competitors; Thou anointed my head with oil, my cup runneth over. Surely goodness and mercy shall follow me all the days of my life and I shall do business in the name of the Lord. Amen.

1. Let there be a breakthrough for me in my transaction, in Jesus' name.

2. Lord, let me have the spirit of favour in this business transaction.

3. I ask for the release of prosperity on my business, in Jesus' name.

4. Let all demonic hindrances to my finances be totally paralysed, in the name of Jesus.

5. I break every circle of failure, in Jesus' name.

6. Let my business be shielded from all evil observers, in Jesus' name.

7.   I claim all my blessings, in the name of Jesus.

8.   Let all business problems receive divine solution in Jesus' name.

9.   Let men go out of their ways to show favour unto me, in Jesus' name.

10.   Lord, let not the lot of the wicked fall upon my business.

RELEASE OF FUNDS INTO BUSINESS

Confession: Deut. 8:18, III John 2, Job 36:11, Col. 2:14,15, Psalm 84:11; 24, Phil. 4:13.

1.   Let the spirit of favour be opened upon me everywhere I go concerning my business, in the name of Jesus.

2.   Father, I ask You, in the name of Jesus, to send ministering spirits to bring in prosperity and funds into my business.

3.   Let men bless me anywhere I go, in the name of Jesus.

4.   I release my business from the clutches of financial hunger, in the name of Jesus.

5. I loose angels, in the mighty name of Jesus, to go and create favour for my company.

6. I bind the spirit in all of the staff members who will try to use evil weapons against me, including lying, gossip, slander and opinionated spirits, in the name of Jesus.

7. Let all financial hindrances be removed, in Jesus' name.

8. I remove my name and those of my customers from the book of financial bankruptcy, in the name of Jesus.

9. Holy Spirit, be the Senior Partner in my business, in Jesus' name.

10. Every good thing presently eluding my business should flow into it, in the mighty name of Jesus.

11. I reject every spirit of financial embarrassment, in the mighty name of Jesus.

12. Father, block every space causing unprofitable leakage to my company, in the mighty name of Jesus.

    Let my company become too hot to handle for dupes and demonic customers, in the name of Jesus.

    Let spiritual magnetic power that attracts wealth and keeps wealth be deposited in my company, in the name of Jesus.

DESTROYING ANTI- PROSPERITY FORCES

Confessions: Gen. 39:3, Deut. 28:3-13, Josh. 1:8, II Chron. 20:20, Neh. 2:19,20, Psalm 1:3, Isa. 55:11, Phil. 4:19.

1. Lord, help me to submit to Your will every day of my life.

2. Lord, cause me to be spiritually and mentally alert in my place of work.

3. Let all my plans and purposes for my business bring honour and glory to the Lord Jesus Christ.

4. Father, let Your angels lift up my business on their hands so that it does not strike its foot against a stone, in the name of Jesus.

5. Let all decisions made on my business be originated by the Holy Ghost, in the name of Jesus.

6. Let the influence of the Holy Ghost be upon every person in this setup, in the name of Jesus.

7. Let increased productivity and profit be the lot of my business, in the name of Jesus.

8. Let my business continue to grow and expand, in the name of Jesus.

9. O Lord, give us direction and guidance at all times in this company.

10. Let the business prosper and have good success, in Jesus' name.

11. Father, let our path grow brighter and brighter until it reaches the full light of the day, in the name of Jesus.

12. I bind every spirit of uncertainty and confusion, in the mighty name of Jesus.

13. I walk out of the realm of failure into the arena of success, in the wonderful name of Jesus.

14. I remove my business from the dominion of the powers of darkness, in the name of Jesus.

15. In Jesus' name, I ask the Father for sufficient legions of the holy angels to bind all satanic forces in my business and in the air overhead, so they will be unable to interfere in my way with its prosperity.

16. I take authority over the binding of the strongman of financial failure, in the name of Jesus.

17. I command the curse and ordination of debt in the business to be nullified, in Jesus' name.

18. Lord, anoint my brain to prosper after the order of Bazaleel the son of Uri, the son of Hur, of the tribe of Judah.

19. Let the anointing of fire be in all my writings, thinking and organization, in the name of Jesus.

20. I stamp out every spirit of anger, lack of co-operation, wrong judgements, contentions and disloyalty amongst all members o f staff, in Jesus' name.

21. Let this business become a channel of blessings and a foundation for other businesses, in Jesus' name.

22. Let the shower of financial revival fall upon the business.

23. Lord, anoint all letters emanating from us for help to be accompanied by divine favour, angelic transportation and positive results.

24. I reverse every curse I have issued against the business, in Jesus' name.

25. Father, in the name of Jesus, assign ministering spirits to go forth and minister on my behalf and bring in trade.

26. Lord, give me the wisdom and ability to understand righteousness and fair dealing in business.

27. Lord, give me grace to remain diligent in acquiring knowledge and skill that in which I am inexperienced.

28. Let my business burst forth and prosper, in the name of Jesus.

29. I declare that the devil will have no control over my finances, in the name of Jesus.

30. I declare that the devil will not be able to steal my finances, in the name of Jesus.

31. Lord, give unto me godly counsel, knowledge and wisdom for managing my finances.

32. Let those who would defraud or cheat me be put to shame and confusion, in the name of Jesus.

33. Let those who would plan to steal from my business be put to shame and confusion in the name of Jesus.

34. Father, make Your face to shine upon me and enlighten me and be gracious unto me, in the name of Jesus.

35. Lord, bestow Your favour upon me, in the name of Jesus.

36. Father, make me a blessing to my family, neighbours and business associates, in the name of Jesus.

37. Lord, pour out upon me the spirit of favour.

38. Father, give me knowledge and skill in all learning and wisdom, in the name of Jesus.

39. Father, bring me to find favour, compassion and loving-kindness with all my business contacts, in the name of Jesus.

40. Lord, cause me to obtain favour in the sight of all who look unto me.

PRAYER FOR DIVINE WISDOM

Confessions: Ps. 118:24; 2 Tim. 1:12; Ps. 91:11; Eph. 3:20; Ps. 16:11; Prov. 3:5-6.

1. Father, let Your wisdom prevail in every meeting held to promote my business, in Jesus' name.

2. Father, help each one in my business to bring forth profitable opinions at appropriate times, in the name of Jesus.

3. Father, help all the members of my business team to operate and flow together as a team, in the name of Jesus.

4.   Let all unproductive and destructive meetings on my business fail to take place, in the name of Jesus.

5.   Lord, help me to hear Your voice and to make the right decisions on my business all the time.

6.   Lord, help me carry out my decision-making accurately and profitably.

7.   Lord, always help me to choose what is best for my business.

8.   Lord, give us new and creative ideas.

9.   Father, let the Holy Spirit show us things to come in the business world.

10.   I claim divine wisdom to enable us to create and develop new products and services, in the name of Jesus.

11.   Lord, help my business to introduce products and services which will be a blessing to people's lives.

12.   Lord, give us innovative concepts and new ideas to enable us to develop newer and better goods and services for our company.

13.   Lord, open ideas to our spirits that can be translated into products and services.

14. Lord, let the positive growth of my business amaze my friends and foes.

15. Lord, direct us to stop planning and working on any project which will waste our time and energy.

16. Let every spirit causing financial wastage depart from my business, in the name of Jesus.

17. Lord, help us to locate a sound financial institution that can and will properly handle our money matters.

PRAYER FOR IMPROVED SALES/SERVICES

Confessions: Ps.46:1; Heb. 1:14; Phil. 4:19; Num 6:25; Det. 28:13; Dan.1:17; Ps. 5:12; Ps. 119:165

1. Lord, bless the efforts of all who are involved in selling our products.

2. Lord, give our people favour with the customers.

3. Father, help our salesmen to understand the needs of our customers.

4. Lord, help our sales representatives never to oversell, but always to efficiently present our products and services.

5. Father, let the Holy Spirit teach us sales promotion and increasing sales techniques.

6. Lord, help us always to remain ahead and not behind.

7. Lord, help us to offer our products in the proper way.

8. Lord, give our salesmen favour as sales representatives.

9. Almighty Father, cause a hunger or request for our goods and services, in Jesus' name.

10. Lord, open new doors and provide new markets for our goods and services.

11. Lord, help us to increase sales and add new markets daily.

PRAYER AGAINST FINANCIAL CRISIS

Confessions: Ps. 115:14; 5:12; Eph. 1:17-18; Lk. 7:41-43.

1. Father, let all who owe my company pay up at the appropriate time, in the name of Jesus.

2. Father, I lift up to you those who are in debt to us. Bless them so that they can pay us, in the name of Jesus.

3. Lord, increase the business of our debtors and make provisions for them to meet their financial obligations.

4. Lord, cause all our debtors with fraudulent intentions to pay up what they owe.

5. Father, send the Holy Spirit to convict all fraudulent debtors that they might repent and make things right, in the name of Jesus.

6. Lord, bring in needed funds through increased sales or decreased expenses to meet all our financial obligations.

7. I come against the spirit of fear, in the name of Jesus.

8. I come against the spirit of anxiety or worry concerning my business situation, in the name of Jesus.

BREAKTHROUGH PRAYER POINTS

Confessions: Job 22:28; Eph. 5:17; Ps. 73:24; Jn. 10:27; 2 Tim. 1:7; Ps. 118:24; 1 Cor. 4:5.

1. Father, guide and direct me to rectify any problem I have with my business.

2. Lord, forgive me for any wrong decision or wrong action or thought I have ever engaged in.

3.   Father, help me to see my mistakes and faults and to do all in my power to overcome and correct them, in Jesus' name.

4.   Father, show me what to do so that crisis would not arise in my business.

5.   Lord, give me the eagle eye and the eyes of Elisha to foresee market situations, in Jesus' name.

6.   Lord, give us wisdom to walk out of any unfavorable business situations.

7.   Father, help me to formulate a plan of recovery to keep us at the top in the name of Jesus.

8.   Lord, send me divine counsellors who can help me with my business.

9.   Lord, always help me to identify evil business traps.

10.   Lord, help me to erect safeguards to prevent business failure.

11.   Lord, send me the right staff who have the same heart and commitment that I have.

12. Lord, let members of our staff be people committed to You and Your word and who operate with integrity and honesty.

13. Lord, let our staff be sincere, above reproach and people who have sure goals and visions and can take sound decisions.

14. Lord, send us staff who will be a healthy perspective to our organisation.

15. Lord, bring me staff that will enhance the company's ability to grow and in turn make profit, in the name of Jesus.

16. Lord, help me to manage the people in my organisation well.

17. Lord, bless the families of my staff financially and physically.

18. Lord, help all members of my staff to control their tongue.

19. Father, give us the anointing to get the job done above and beyond our own strength, abilities, gifts and talents.

20. Lord, impart to all members of staff everything they need to perform their duties with joy and excellence.

21. If the right persons for our work are not currently here, Lord bring them here.

22. Help us, Lord, to serve our customers better.

23. Help us Lord to be more sensitive to the needs of our customers and more responsible to their desires and wants.

24. Lord, help us to be on the lookout for ways to provide better products and services.

25. Lord, help me to yield to the Holy Spirit whenever I encounter circumstances beyond my knowledge.

26. In the mighty name of Jesus, I claim the following:

    (a) Good reputation.

    (b) Favour with clients and customers.

    (c) Abundant prosperity.

    (d) Divine wisdom for those who occupy important decision-making positions.

    (e) Increased sales and services and expanded markets.

    (f) New product ideas and new servicing concepts.

27.   Lord, help me to do my very best at all times.

28.   Let all our workers perform their duties with a spirit of excellence.

29.   Let all our workers fulfill their duties to the best of their ability.

30.   I break myself and my workers loose from unproductive habits in Jesus' name.

31.   Lord, let all our workers receive the enabling power to plan their day and pay attention to their duties.

32.   Father, I dedicate and consecrate my business to You, in Jesus' name.

CREATING GOOD WORKING RELATIONSHIP

Confessions: 1 Samuel 2:26; Job 10:12; Ps. 5:12; Prov. 3:4; 21:1; Job 22:28; Phil. 4:13.

1.   I command every spirit working against me in the heart of my boss to be bound and to leave, in the name of Jesus.

2.   I bind every spirit of career destruction, in the name of Jesus.

3. I break myself loose from every curse of work disruption, in the name of Jesus.

4. Father Lord, loose Your angels to go and create favour for me before my boss and other members of my department.

5. I bind the spirits in all the personnel who would try to use evil against me, including lying, gossip and slander, in the name of Jesus.

6. Father, loose Your angels to go and create favour with my boss and to secure my position, in the name of Jesus.

7. I receive power to fight the enemy and drive him back in my life, job, finances and home, in the name of Jesus.

8. Let every decision taken on my case be completely favourable to me, in Jesus' name.

9. I decree breakthroughs in all my business endeavours, in the name of Jesus.

MAKE YOUR WAY PLAIN BEFORE MY FACE

Confessions: Deut. 29:29; Ps. 5:8; 25:14; Dan. 2:22; Eph. 1:17.

1.   Thank God for the revelation power of the Holy Spirit.

2.   O Lord, give unto me the Spirit of revelation and wisdom in the knowledge of Yourself.

3.   O Lord, make Your way plain before my face on this issue.

4.   O Lord, remove spiritual cataract from my eyes.

5.   O Lord, forgive me for every false motive or thought that has ever been formed in my heart since the day I was born.

6.   O Lord, forgive me for any lie that I have ever told against any person, system or organisation.

7.   O Lord, deliver me from the bondage and sin of spiritual laziness.

8.   O Lord, open up my eyes to see all I should on this issue.

9.   O Lord, teach me deep and secret things.

10. O Lord, reveal to me every secret behind any problem that I have.

11. O Lord, bring to light every thing planned against me in darkness.

12. O Lord, ignite and revive my beneficial potentials.

13. O Lord, give me divine wisdom to operate my life.

14. O Lord, let every veil preventing me from having plain spiritual vision be removed.

15. O Lord, give unto me the spirit of revelation and wisdom in the knowledge of You.

16. O Lord, open my spiritual understanding.

17. O Lord, let me know all I should know about this issue.

18. O Lord, reveal to me every secret behind the particular issue, whether beneficial or not.

19. O Lord, remove from me any persistent buried grudges, half acknowledged enmity against anyone and every other thing that can block my spiritual vision.

20. O Lord, teach me to know that which is worth knowing and love that which is worth loving and to dislike whatsoever is not pleasing to Your eyes.

21. O Lord, make me a vessel capable of knowing Your secret things.

22. Father, in the name of Jesus, I ask to know Your mind about . . . (*slot in the appropriate situation*) situation.

23. Let the spirit of prophesy and revelation fall upon the totality of my being, in the name of Jesus.

24. Holy Spirit, reveal deep and secret things to m e about . . ., in the name of Jesus.

25. I bind every demon that pollutes spiritual vision and dreams, in the name of Jesus.

26. Let every dirt blocking my communication pipe with the living God be washed clean with the blood of Jesus, in Jesus' name.

27. I receive power to operate with sharp spiritual eyes that cannot be deceived, in the name of Jesus.

28. Let the glory and the power of the Almighty God, fall upon my life in a mighty way, in the name of Jesus.

29. I remove my name from the book of those who grope and stumble in darkness, in the name of Jesus.

30. Divine revelations, spiritual visions, dreams and information will not become scarce commodities in my life, in the name of Jesus.

31. I drink to the full in the well of salvation and anointing, in the name of Jesus.

32. O God, to whom no secret is hidden, make known unto me whether . . . (*mention the name of the thing*) is Your choice for me, in the name of Jesus.

33. Let every idol present consciously or unconsciously, in my heart concerning this issue be melted away by the fire of the Holy Spirit, in the name of Jesus.

34. I refuse to fall under the manipulation of the spirits of confusion, in the name of Jesus.

35. I refuse to make foundational mistakes in my decision, in the name of Jesus.

36. Father Lord, guide and direct me in knowing Your mind on this particular issue, in the name of Jesus.

37. I stand against all satanic attachments that may seek to confuse my decision, in the name of Jesus.

38. If . . . (*mention the name of the thing*) is not for me, O Lord, redirect my steps.

39.   I bind the activities of . . . (*pick from the list below*) in m y
       life, in the name of Jesus.

       - lust   - ungodly infatuation

       - ungodly family pressure

       - demonic manipulation in dreams and visions

       - attachment to the wrong choice

       - confusing revelations

       - spiritual blindness and deafness

       - unprofitable advice   - ungodly impatience

40.   O God, You who reveals secret things, make known
       unto me Your choice for me in this issue, in the name of
       Jesus.

41.   Holy Spirit, open my eyes and help me to make the right
       decision, in the name of Jesus.

42.   Thank You Jesus for Your presence and the good
       testimonies that will follow.

43.   Pray in the spirit for at least 15 minutes.

9

DELIVERANCE FOR INANIMATE OBJECTS

First, I want you to read the testimony of a white-man who was attending a traditional church, where they did not believe that any trouble could be caused by the devil. They believed that you just went your own way and the devil went his own way.

One day, somebody invited this white-man to a workshop whose topic was "Battling the host of Hell." That topic sounded as fiction to the white-man. Anyway, he attended and listened to what was being said. He knew he had been having problems, which the church he was going had no solution.

After the workshop, he decided to experiment on the things he learnt. This is the report of the experiment:

I went to this workshop, I listened to the teachings about how to anoint your place of work and how to bind and loose spirits over your job. Because my boss is not a Christian, the enemy had a lot of opportunity to use him against me. The devil was trying hard to make me lose my job, so I decided as taught in the seminar to counter attack.

The first night I took a bottle of olive oil, which I had prayed on, and I walked the entire breadth and length of the place where I work and I anointed every door in the name of the Lord Jesus Christ. I also commanded that every evil spirit should be bound and leave, especially those who were trying to take my job, such as witchcraft spirit and spirit of destruction. He first operated outside the building.

Next, I went inside the building. I anointed the office of each department which affected my job. I loose angels in the name of the Lord Jesus Christ to create favour for my department. I bind every spirit over each department which could affect my own department. I also bound the spirit in all of the management and personnel which may like to use evil against me, including spirit of lying, gossip and slander. I loose angels to create favour for me with my boss and to secure my position in the company.

This I did every night and soon I began to notice a change in the production output of my own department. As it began to increase, this caused great favour with my supervisor who gradually began to change his opinion about me. The angels continued to cause my department to flow smoother and it consistently raised the production.

On the day of our first management meeting, my boss complimented me and my department. He had never been known to compliment anyone before.

"I give all the credit and glory to the Lord and Saviour Jesus Christ for all the victory and I thank God for the power to fight the enemy and draw him back, not only in my life, but in my job and finances."

This is the testimony of a man who was not ready to allow himself to be cheated or for the spirit of financial destruction to enter his job. From the testimony there are big lessons to be learnt.

One big lesson here is that the spirit working against your interest may be hiding inside inanimate objects in your place of work, or in a lifeless object in your home.

The second lesson is that a curse may be placed on somebody through inanimate objects. Somebody may say: "As far as this man touches this object, his work will not prosper. As far as he is sitting on this chair, he will never make progress." A curse may be pronounced thus: "let everyone using this chair or carpet be against this brother." In such an instance, unless the individual is spiritually discerning enough, he would not understand the reason everybody is against him.

This is why, when you (a believer) start to work in a new place, you should not take anything for granted. It is important to carry out spiritual cleansing of your new office\workshop \stall\shop. You must extend your cleansing operations to the existing furniture.

The third lesson is that if you do not take quick and aggressive action, the way this man has taken, your enemy will push you out of your place of benefit and you will think it is from God or it is by coincidence.

I want this to be clear in your spirit before we move on: one of the problems we have with Christianity in this country is that many Christians do not realise that ministries must address indigenous problems. It is high time we began to see the evil spirits operating here as indigenous ones and that they act, afflict and dribble people according to our customs and traditions.

This is Nigeria in Africa, not in America; and if we 'Americanise' our ministry, it will not be functional against the troubles of the black man. Contaminated property and materials cause serious problem here and if curses or wicked spirits that are against you are attached to inanimate objects, they can cause serious problems in several ways: they may be the source of attack for you in the house or in your place of work.

They may be the source of affliction or of things energising evil influence in those places. These materials may even be initiating people into evil associations.

They may be a source of oppression or instrument of depression; a person may notice that whenever he enters an environment, he becomes unhappy.

They may be an instrument that will persuade somebody to do evil. If you have objects dedicated to demons in your possession, the best action is to destroy them. It is very important that believers carry out spiritual inspections on fairly used cars, clothes, houses, etc. If the former owners were demonic, or involved in serious bondage, or in serious sin, they will leave the evil spirits behind. They will linger behind and cause trouble for the new owner.

This is how people purchase things that swallow their money. Thank God for fairly used cars. But always remember to cleanse them before use since you may not know the true spiritual state of their former owners. A car may need deliverance, and it is the same for a second-hand cloth, etc.

That equipment which has been having problem may need deliverance. This is why after the Anointing Service was held, some people anointed non-functional equipment and they started to function. Something evil was preventing the equipment from functioning. Also, that your flat may need deliverance, especially if the house was built with bloody or unrighteous money.

Also know and recognize that any prayer that anybody is saying to personalities different from God the Father, God the Son and God the Holy Spirit, is a prayer to demon. If you move to any house where they pray to something other than God, you may be experiencing trouble until you minister deliverance to that house.

Very often, those strange prayers get answers and those who pray them think that the answers are from God, but God is not in them.

You may move into a new apartment only to discover that you are not able to sleep, or that you are getting poorer and poorer. There may be a strange thing within this house reversing your fullness. Then you should take some spiritual actions as that white man did.

It is not that black people do not have testimonies, I purposely presented that of a white-man so that you will know that no country is free from the evils perpetrated by satan.

Do you know that some sisters who are praying for husband already have three husbands and are just asking for one extra? You will say how would they do that. They bought three different wedding rings in the market. So they have been married to three different spirit husbands. Now they are looking for number four, an ordinary human being. They bought the rings for decoration, not knowing that some spirits are attached to them.

Do you know why many try to sell things and find that they do not sell? Sometimes those things need deliverance.

Do you know why transporters have a lot of headache? It is because, for example at a given terminal, 14 passengers who board a bus are made up of five witches, two herbalists, one magician and other people of similar demonic deposition. It is automatic that this vehicle will have problems because of the heavy spiritual load.

So, if you are to be involved in transportation business, you must learn the secret of regularly anointing your vehicles. I call this spiritual disinfectant.

Many people have to cleanse their property. When you are constructing your house and constructors on the site are cursing people, the house will be possessed.

When you have an uncompleted building and school girls and school boys go there to commit fornication, the house will be cursed.

The Bible says, "My people are destroyed for lack of knowledge," (Hosea 4:6). A whole land may be under a curse because it was forcibly taken from the rightful owner. That land will need deliverance.

Deuteronomy 7:26: Neither shall thou bring an abomination into thine house, lest thou be a cursed thing like it, but thou shall utterly detest it and thou shall utterly abhor it: for it is a cursed thing.

This means that if you bring any cursed item into your house, you become cursed by it.

Joshua 7:11: Israel has sinned and they have also transgressed my covenant which I commanded them; for they have even taken of the accursed thing, and have also stolen, and dissembled also, and they have put it even among their own staff.

Verse 12: Therefore the children of Israel could not stand before their enemies, but turned their backs before their enemies, because they were accursed, neither will I be with you anymore, except ye destroy the accursed from among you.

A single person, just one man, stole a Babylonian garment that a curse was upon and brought it to a camp of about three million people and that single garment put the whole people in trouble and God said, "I will not be satisfied until you destroy it."

It is important to first get people delivered before they go and do deliverance for their property. Otherwise, they will go back and re-contaminate the property with their own demons.

Wherever Christians are present, whether at home or in an office or hotel, there is a shelter of protection against evil forces. But wicked forces can pollute places with their unholy presence. Such pollution usually occurs when, for example, a building is used for immoral acts or prostitution, selling of dangerous drugs, occultic activities, alcoholism, etc.

These bad spirits linger on long after those who caused them to enter have left, hoping to prey upon unsuspecting newcomers.

CLEANSING PROCESS

How then do you cleanse your home, your office, your car, land, farm, properties of evil spirits?

- First, prepare yourself by fasting and prayer and by studying the word of God. Do at least one day fast. This first stage is preparation.

- Secondly, find a good prayer partner, if possible, to go along with you. Jesus sent His disciples two by two.

- Thirdly, you must have at least the following nine scriptures in your memory or written out for the attack. You must know them:

  - Revelation 12:11: And they overcame him by the blood of the Lamb, and by the word of their testimony; and they loved not their lives unto the death.

  - Revelation 22:3: And there shall be no more curse: but the throne of God and of the Lamb shall be in it; and his servants shall serve Him:

- Colossians 2:14,15: Blotting out the handwriting of ordinances that was against us, which w as contrary to us, and took it out of the way, nailing it to His cross; And having spoiled principalities and powers, He made a shew of them openly, triumphing over them in it.

- Galatians 3:13,14: Christ hath redeemed us from the curse of the law, being made a curse for us: for it is written, Cursed is every one that hangeth on a tree: That the blessing of Abraham might come on the Gentiles through Jesus Christ; that we might receive the promise through faith.

- Deuteronomy 21:23: His body shall not remain all night upon the tree, but thou shalt in any wise bury him that day; (for he that is hanged is accursed of God;) that thy land be not defiled, which the LORD thy God giveth thee for an inheritance.

- Deuteronomy 32:5: They have corrupted themselves, their spot is not the spot of his children: they are a perverse and crooked generation.

- Numbers 23 :8: How shall I curse, whom God hath not cursed? or how shall I defy, whom the LORD hath not defied?

- Numbers 23:23: Surely there is no enchantment against Jacob, neither is there any divination against Israel: according to this time it shall be said of Jacob and of Israel, What hath God wrought!

- II Samuel 7:29: Therefore now let it please thee to bless the house of thy servant, that it may continue for ever before thee: for thou, O Lord God, hast spoken it: and with thy blessing let the house of thy servant be blessed for ever.

- Luke 10:19: Behold, I give unto you power to tread on serpents and scorpions, and over all the power of the enemy: and nothing shall by any means hurt you.

With these scriptures you must be ready to do the work.

• In addition, when you move into the environment, you read these scriptures out loud, you and your partner, in unison or separately.

• Lastly, you pray for discernment by asking the Holy Spirit to reveal to you where you will lay your hands. Have in your possession a bottle of olive oil and if possible some anointed handkerchiefs. The scriptures for this are found in Mark 6:13: "And they cast out many devils, and anointed with oil many that were sick, and healed them."

And in James 5:14: "Is any sick among you? let him call for the elders of the church; and let them pray over him, anointing him with oil in the name of the Lord."

Also in Acts 19:11, 12: "And God wrought special miracles by the hands of Paul." "So that from his body were brought unto the sick handkerchiefs or aprons, and diseases departed from them."

THE ANOINTING AND PRAYER

When you pray on the olive oil or lay your hands on the handkerchiefs, asking God to anoint them, the power of God enters into the two items. Wherever they are used, evil spirits must depart.

Now, begin to attack all the evil powers around. Verbally denounce satan and all his host and claim your authority over them as a believer. Walk around the place, praying, commanding the spirits to depart, touching where the Spirit of God directs you to touch after dipping your hand in the anointing oil.

If strange things have been happening in that house or to that machine or instrument, then call out the specific spirits. It is sufficient to call them by the name of the evil activities they sponsor. It may be the spirit of poverty, witchcraft, familiar spirits, etc. Call them out and bind them.

When you finish praying as described above, then pray a wall of fire around those things, plead the blood of Jesus on them and ask for the angels of God to be stationed in the place.

If it is a home, start by anointing the doors, lintels and windows. You can also anoint things like toys, cars, wardrobes, cupboards and other equipment in the house. Then begin to praise the Lord for the victory.

Finally, if you have books and objects associated with witchcraft, astrology, good-luck charms, occultic books, Christian science literature, books on strange uses of the Psalms, demonic prayer uniforms, prayer candles and incense, etc, ensure that they are destroyed by setting them on fire. God bless you as you do so, in Jesus' name.

Publications by Dr. D. K. Olukoya

1. Be Prepared
2. Breakthrough Prayers For Business Professionals
3. Brokenness
4. Criminals In The House of God
5. Dealing With Local Satanic Technology
6. Dealing With Witchcraft Barbers
7. Dealing With Hidden Curses
8. Dealing With The Evil Powers of Your Father's House
9. Dealing With Unprofitable Roots
10. Deliverance: God's Medicine Bottle
11. Deliverance By Fire
12. Deliverance From Spirit Husband And Spirit Wife
13. Deliverance of The Conscience
14. Deliverance of The Head
15. Drawers of Power From The Heavenlies
16. Dominion Prosperity
17. Evil Appetite
18. Fasting And Prayer
19. Failure In The School Of Prayer
20. For We Wrestle . . .
21. Holy Cry
22. Holy Fever
23. How To Obtain Personal Deliverance (Second Edition)
24. Limiting God
25. Meat For Champions
26. Overpowering Witchcraft
27. Personal Spiritual Check-up
28. Power Against Coffin Spirits

ALL OBTAINABLE AT:

* **MFM International Bookshop,** 13, Olasimbo Street, Onike, Yaba.

* **MFM Press Bookstore,** 54, Akeju Street, Off Shipeolu Street, Onipanu, Lagos.

* **The Battle Cry Christian Ministries,** 322, Herbert Macaulay Way, Sabo, Yaba, Lagos.

* **IPFY Music Konnections Limited,** 48, Opebi Road, Salvation Bus Stop (234-1-4719471, 234-8033056093)

* **All MFM Church branches nationwide (www.mountain-of-fire.com) and Christian bookstores.**